On Four Fronts With the Royal Naval Division

MAJOR-GENERAL SIR ARCHIBALD PARIS,
K.C.B., R.M.A.

On Four Fronts With the Royal Naval Division

During the First World War
1914-1918

Geoffrey Sparrow
J. N. MacBean Ross

LEONAUR

On Four Fronts With the Royal Naval Division
During the First World War 1914-1918
by Geoffrey Sparrow
and
J. N. MacBean Ross

First published under the title
On Four Fronts With the Royal Naval Division

Leonaur is an imprint of Oakpast Ltd

Copyright in this form © 2011 Oakpast Ltd

ISBN: 978-0-85706-715-9 (hardcover)
ISBN: 978-0-85706-716-6 (softcover)

http://www.leonaur.com

Publisher's Notes

Contents

To the Officers, Noncommissioned Officers, and Men of the Royal Naval Division, this book is dedicated as a token of deep admiration and affectionate regard by their sincere friends

The Authors

Foreword

By Surgeon-General Sir James Porter, K.C.B., K.C.M.G., R.N.

The authors have given us at first hand in fascinating form an absorbing and realistic narrative of stirring times in the annals of the Royal Naval Division. They have seen with their own observant eyes, and been themselves a part of all they describe in many lands. Accuracy is the dominant note through all their graphic pen and pencil pictures.

It was my privilege to see this wonderful division in the making when the raw material was composed of an assortment of men strangely varied, but of a high physical standard. They were all keen to learn, the war being urgent and dispatch necessary. Hence in a marvellously short time they became transformed by their Marine and Naval Instructors into the wonderful fighting-men portrayed in these pages. Of good physique to start with, their training imbued them with the ready resource of the sailor and the precision of the soldier.

The authors take us pleasantly and with light touch through ever changing scenes from the Antwerp expedition, through the Homeric combats of Gallipoli, to Salonica and the Isles of Greece with their poisonous, malarial climate, to the muddy, bloodstained trenches of the Western Front. Hard fighting made them happy, and the ever changing climate, from blizzard to blazing sunshine, never dulled their cheery spirits. They have done well in recording what at the time was common knowledge amongst all in Gallipoli, that the '*Turk was a clean fighter*,' because he was still his old self, uncontaminated by methods of *Kultur*.

One wishes the authors had said more about the everlasting miracle of the evacuation of the Gallipoli Peninsula. That feat we owe to the military genius of General Sir Charles Munro, splendidly supported by Admirals Sir John de Robeck, Sir Rosslyn Wemyss, and Sir

Roger Keyes—all today men of light and leading, and sheet anchors of their country. On the eve of the evacuation there was a general outside consensus of opinion amongst sailors and soldiers on the spot that 40 *per cent*, of casualties might reasonably be expected in the operation of removing our many thousands of men from these perilous beaches washed by a turbulent sea, beaten upon by adverse winds and swept by the enemy's guns. Happily the unofficial experts turned out to be all wrong, and the clearance was effected with practically no loss of life. The feat will pass into history as a great and successful military operation, and a teaching example of what perfect co-operation between navy and army can achieve when directed by trained and experienced master minds working in complete harmony one with the other.

The chapter on the duties of a battalion medical officer is full of good and practical things, *e.g.* the rum ration. The attacks on it by total abstinence extremists are of old standing, and repeat themselves periodically. The truth is that the small daily tot of rum, issued under Service conditions, cannot possibly harm any adult human being. On the contrary, it is within the writer's personal experience, and of that of thousands who have been under his care, that at the end of a hard day in the field a tot of rum comforts, soothes, and supports the weary and worn.

It is sad to read in these pages that suppuration in wounds is so common. In South Africa it was the exception, possibly because the pure air and virgin soil of the *veldt* were free from the germs of disease which swarm in the cultivated lands of France and under the insanitary conditions ever present in the Eastern Mediterranean.

Readers will find much easily assimilated instruction in these brightly written pages. May the book meet with the success it so richly deserves!

James Porter.

Preface

By Major-General Sir Archibald Paris, K.C.B., R.M.A.

I am asked to write a preface to this entertaining work. It speaks for itself as a personal narrative of thrilling adventures.

I am glad to have this opportunity to express my high appreciation of the loyal assistance given by all ranks of the division, frequently under most difficult circumstances. The medical arrangements, especially during the Gallipoli Campaign, when everything had to be improvised, were the admiration of all.

The authors have certainly seen more of the World War than is the fortune of most.

The thousands of gallant comrades who have fallen in the great cause, and whose loss we all deeply mourn, created an '*esprit*' which the division has well maintained.

I am indeed proud to have had for just over two years the command of such a fine body of men.

The peculiar difficulties of modern warfare are common to all newly formed units, but in addition we were from almost the first day in a constant state of reorganisation, due to the fact that the backbone of the division consisted of men trained—more or less—for sea service, and as admiralty requirements grew, so the comb had to be applied until there were very few 'ratings' left, and the gaps could not be filled from naval sources.

I notice a page giving a list of honours awarded. It is perhaps unnecessary to say that though heartily congratulating the numerous recipients, it is certainly a fact that not a half of those who deserved and earned honours and rewards have got them. This is inevitable, when war is on such a colossal scale.

A. Paris.

63RD (ROYAL NAVAL) DIVISION

Decorations Awarded up to 13th June 1918 [1]

Victoria Cross	3
Distinguished Service Cross	17
Military Cross	137
Bar to Military Cross	8
Second Bar to Military Cross	1
K.C.B.	1
C.B.	9
C.M.G	10
D.S.O	42
Bar to D.S.O	4
Second Bar to D.S.O.	1
Military Medal	555
Bar to Military Medal	23
Second Bar to Military Medal	1
Conspicuous Gallantry Medal	23
Distinguished Conduct Medal	53
Bar to Distinguished Conduct Medal	1
Distinguished Service Medal	79
Meritorious Service Medal	9
Albert Medal	1
Foreign Orders and Decorations	54
Total	1032

1. We are indebted to Lieutenant-Colonel Simpson, R.M.L.I., O.C. Records, for kindly supplying these figures, and for much other valuable assistance.

Authors' Preface

In presenting these rambling notes for the perusal of an indulgent public, we feel we have much to apologise for. Our only excuse is the pressing request of numerous friends, who while rightly thinking that the doings of the Royal Naval Division are worthy of record, quite erroneously imagine that we are capable of describing them as they deserve to be described.

We give our impressions for what they are worth, knowing full well that they are disconnected, scrappy, and open to much criticism, but at the same time they represent life as we found it during those never-to-be-forgotten days, in which we had the privilege of being attached to the Royal Naval Division.

Throughout we have attempted to leave the field of strategy entirely alone, and to confine ourselves to actual facts. Numerous gallant episodes perforce remain unmentioned, as we are merely recording events which came under our notice, and do not wish our story to be regarded in any sense as a chronological statement of all the doings of the division.

To our many friends, with whom we served, we tender our grateful thanks for much assistance and information, and to Dr. Fothergill, the well-known Scottish artist, for great technical assistance in preparing this book for the press.

Though the Royal Naval Division is '*without a divine poet to chronicle its deeds,*' still those of us who are left would not willingly forget them.

WAITING FOR SOMETHING TO TURN UP

CHAPTER 1

The Formation and Constitution of the R.N.D.

'E isn't one o' the reg'lar line, nor 'e isn't one o' the crew,
'E's a kind of a giddy harumphrodite—soldier and sailor too.

Kipling.

How many of us at the outbreak of war joined up quickly lest it should come to an end before we had a chance of participating in it? Bets were freely exchanged, even amongst Service men, that all would be over by Christmas 1914, and here it is in its fifth year, having outlived so many of these gallant optimists.

After many vicissitudes I was duly enrolled in His Majesty's Navy as a temporary surgeon, and very soon was sent to one of our large naval depots, where I met many others in circumstances similar to mine. Of course we were merely there for disposal and so had little or nothing to do. The majority, like Micawber, were waiting for something to turn up. There are two ways of doing this—one merely to wait and the other continually to pester the authorities for a job. Some apparently thought they were specially qualified in the eyes of the gods for a life on the ocean wave, mainly because they had spent so much of their spare time investigating the backwaters of the Thames or for some other equally illogical reason.

These individuals were constantly applying for a ship but, such is fate, usually found themselves appointed to some shore billet far removed from the sea they loved so well. Some, indeed, became such a nuisance to the already overworked authorities that an order was issued stating that officers would serve their country best by ceasing to apply for posts to which they might think themselves suited.'

After only thirty-six hours in depot I was appointed to the Royal Naval Camp at Walmer, and duly arrived there with three others of my professional *confrères* to commence duty with the then unknown R.N.D.

The Royal Naval Division had only been formed for a few weeks, and the 1st Brigade, consisting of the Collingwood, Hawke, Benbow, and Drake Battalions, was under canvas on Walmer Downs, two miles from Deal. The 2nd Brigade, composed of the Howe, Hood, Anson, and Nelson Battalions, was at Bettysanger, and the 3rd or Royal Marine Brigade formed by the Portsmouth, Plymouth, Chatham, and Deal Battalions, was stationed at Friedown Camp.

The scene on the Downs, where all three brigades were training hard, was, to my civilian eye, full of interest. The predominant note was blue, with here and there a splash of khaki—outfitters' experiments in khaki naval uniform. The latter, as far as officers were concerned, consisted of a tunic built on the plan of the ordinary blue monkey jacket, but, as a concession to our military occupation, a Sam Brown belt was worn. Just a few compromised by wearing a blue monkey jacket with khaki breeches and pigskin leggings. The cap adopted by most was the ordinary naval one with a khaki cap cover. The men, as a whole, wore blue shore-going rig, though a small number were the proud possessors of a khaki uniform with black naval buttons and a khaki cap adorned with a black ribband bearing the legend 'Royal Naval Division.'

These few remarks regarding our clothing are made, not because we were over proud of it, but because people who read the papers in those days seemed to get the impression that the R.N.D. was naked, or at any rate that one ambulatory organ was encased in a blue, bell-bottomed trouser leg, whilst the other rejoiced in khaki and a ragged *puttee*.

No doubt some of us presented a somewhat variegated appearance, but this only tended to increase the interest of the local inhabitants, though it must have been a matter of some astonishment to the active service members of the division. An unfailing source of amusement to all was the occasional glimpse of some unfortunate person learning to ride; a certain proportion of the officers of a battalion have to ride, and this proportion was generally in excess of those who were able. The equestrian feats of a certain officer who usually had some excuse why he should not ride still live in the memories of all who knew him. 'How dare you bring me a horse that is ill?' he demanded

THE R.N.D. UNIFORM
AT ANTWERP

THE R.N.D. UNIFORM AS THE
GENERAL PUBLIC BELIEVED
IT TO BE

ROYAL MARINE UNIFORM OF
1664

of his inoffensive little groom, somewhat nervously eyeing a curious excrescence, which for many years had adorned the nasal organ of Bucephalus. However, he finally mounted and soon was careering over the parade ground, to the very audible annoyance of his commanding officer and to the intense amusement of the rest of us. His reckless course was only stemmed by becoming entangled in the guy ropes of the tents.

I must admit that there were few horses in our lines which exceeded the speed limit, though personally I was provided with a strange animal who totally refused to answer to the helm and had only two paces—dead slow and full speed ahead.

We doctors, like the rest, were soon hard at work treating influenza, sore feet and other minor ailments, due to the sudden change from a sedentary occupation to a strenuous camp life. At first men came to us out of pure curiosity, just as they crowd to see the fat boy of Peckham at an exhibition side show, but later they came in real earnest. Many complained that only 'orficers 'as habdomens and men merely stomicks,' but on the whole we got on very well together, and to do them justice, after the first novelty had worn off, they rarely came to us unless they were in real need of treatment. Malingering was a distinct rarity and only occurred when there was not enough to do.

A much busier department than ours was that of the Quartermaster's Stores. The text of the efficient Q.M. is *He that hath not, from him shall be taken away even that which he hath,* and so, many of the R.N.V.R. ratings who arrived with all their peace-time gear were quickly deprived of much that would be of little use to them on active service.

Most of the men, however, before they went to Antwerp, were at least equipped with rifles, bayonets, *bandoliers*, and other offensive implements, and I cannot say I ever saw a bayonet tied on with string, although at the time this fact was confidently stated in the newspapers.

The constitution of the Royal Naval Division is a subject on which there is much ignorance amongst the public. It is not very long ago since a prominent Member of Parliament referred to us as 'a new *battalion* consisting largely of *Marines.*'

On the outbreak of war the Royal Fleet Reserve (men who had formerly been in the Royal Navy), the Royal Naval Reserve (men belonging to the merchant service), and the Royal Naval Volunteer Reserve (landsmen who had had a certain amount of sea training) were automatically mobilised.

The Right Honourable Winston Churchill, at that time First Lord of the Admiralty, found he had more men at his disposal than were required for immediate service at sea, and so the Royal Naval Division was formed. It was given at the time wide publicity in the press—an attention it failed to receive during the Dardanelles campaign, but regained by sheer merit after coming to France. Like two of the campaigns in which it was engaged its conception was possibly ill-judged, but that, like the campaigns, is now a matter of the past and does not concern us here. The fact, however, remains, that from the first the R.N.D. was a fine body of men, and at last, after many months of active service in Gallipoli and France, is recognised by all as one of our finest fighting divisions. Though modelled on the plan of an army division, it was not until after our return from Antwerp that it had any divisional troops, *i.e.* engineers, field ambulances, etc., and not until reaching France any divisional artillery. Of the three brigades two were recruited from R.F.R., R.N.R., and R.N.V.R. ratings and led by R.N.V.R. officers and a few retired R.N. and Guards officers. The third brigade consisted of Royal Marine Light Infantry—a corps which has served in all parts of the world, and distinguished itself in every campaign since its formation in 1664.

As the ordinary civilian knows so little of the Royal Marines it may be instructive to point out here how and when they came into being.

By a special Order in Council of 1664 a force of 1200 soldiers in six companies was raised for sea service during the Dutch War. In all probability they were recruited from the London Trained Bands, and there is evidence of this in the fact that the Royal Marines, 3rd Grenadier Guards, East Kents, and the London Militia alone have the privilege of marching through London with fixed bayonets.

In 1684 an organised battalion of Marines was formed and known as H.R.H. the Duke of York and Albany's Maritime Regiment of Foot, or the Lord High Admiral's Regiment of Foot. Several other maritime regiments were successively raised and disbanded, and in 1702 Queen Anne raised six regiments and added them to the army as a marine corps, while appointing six existing regiments for sea service. Twelve years later the corps was again disbanded, three battalions only remaining—the 30th, 31st, and 32nd, of the line.

In 1755 five thousand men were raised in fifty companies and placed under the naval authorities to be stationed at Chatham, Portsmouth, and Plymouth, and in 1805 a Woolwich Division was added.

By an Order in Council, May 18th, 1804, 'in consequence of the inconvenience of embarking the Royal Artillery,' one company of Marine Artillery was formed out of each division, and in 1862 the Artillery was separated from the Light Infantry, and stationed at Fort Cumberland, Portsmouth. It was removed in 1869 to Eastney.

The uniform of 1664 shown in the accompanying illustration consists of a canary yellow coat with red cuffs, red breeches and stockings, and a black hat trimmed with gold braid.

It must be remembered that, though the Naval Brigades had no previous military experience, the four Royal Marine Battalions were regulars, and their efficiency quite equalled that of any troops in the British Army.

Our divisional commander was Major General Sir Archibald Paris, K.C.B. (who succeeded Sir George Ashton [sick] in September 1914), whilst two brigades were commanded by commodores, and the Royal Marine Brigade by a brigadier-general. That it presented a multitude of picturesque types is not to be wondered at, when it is remembered there were pensioners, short service men, and recruits from marine depots; fleet reservists, chiefly stokers, who had served for seven years and then joined the R.F.R.; naval reservists from the merchant service and fishing villages, many hailing from the North of Scotland and speaking a language totally unintelligible to the Southerner; the naval volunteers from the Clyde, Tyne, Mersey, Sussex, London, and Bristol Divisions, and last but not least, about two thousand of Kitchener's first hundred thousand. In spite of their seeming incompatibility these men soon became friends, and owing to their remarkably fine physique and intelligence quickly became smart on parade and efficient in their duties. It was anticipated that the division would be in training for about six months before going on active service, but the war developed in a somewhat abrupt manner by the very rapid progress of events in Belgium, and we had to go long before it was primarily intended.

Our busy though undisturbed life of camp routine was constantly interrupted by 'buzzes.' As the reader may not fully understand what the term 'buzz' means, I shall attempt to define it. A 'buzz' is a report of untraceable origin; though occasionally entirely false it usually has a small molecule of truth in its composition; it is sometimes probable, more often highly improbable; it is always widely believed and spreads from mouth to mouth with amazing rapidity. You meet 'buzzes' everywhere—in shell-holes, trenches, dugouts, rest-billets, hospitals, and many other places both at home and abroad. A knowing individual, bursting with information, tells you he has it on the highest authority that we have advanced so many miles in such and such a sector. He knows to a man how many Boches have been killed and captured, what our losses were, and so minutely describes various gruesome and revolting details that the unwary are apt to believe his story implicitly, and pass it on to their friends, still further embroidered by the vagaries of an active imagination.

Some affirmed we were to garrison St. Helena, others that we were to capture Heligoland, many believed we were going to France, and a few authoritatively stated we were to finish our training at Dunkirk—in fact, anything sensational found credence. Gradually the 'buzzes' became so improbable that the camp ultimately settled down into a state of pronounced scepticism from which it was, from time to time, aroused by the Royal Marine Brigade taking a trip across the Channel.

On August 26th, 1914, they were ordered to Ostend and spent four strenuous days digging defensive trenches from the Mariakerke-Bruges Railway to the coast. Again, on September 19th, they were hurried across to Dunkirk, where they were joined by a mixed force under Commander Sampson, D.S.O., R.N., which had already been in action with Uhlan patrols in the vicinity of Arras, Douai, and Lille. On September 28th the Portsmouth Battalion, under Lieutenant-Colonel Luard, R.M.L.I., was ordered to Lille to cover the retirement of the French at Douai, Tournai, and Orchies, and on September 30th the remainder of the brigade was sent to the little town of Cassel.

On October 3rd we were awakened with the news that at last the division, as a whole, was going on active service, and that camp was to be struck immediately—not at all a pleasant thing to hear at 5 o'clock in the morning. The scene was indescribable. Packing and unpacking was the order of the day. Some feared they had not enough gear, others, knowing full well they had too much, could not decide whether to pack or part with it; and after all what can one do with a large tin bath, a chest of drawers, a bed, and a looking-glass when suddenly ordered on active service!

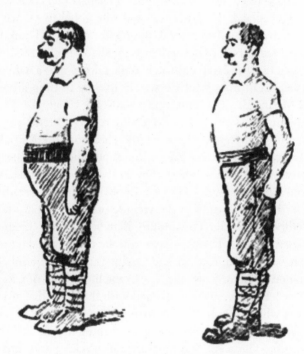

BEFORE AND AFTER PHYSICAL DRILL

ANTWERP—OCTOBER 1914

ROYAL NAVAL DIVISION

(Major-General Paris, C.B., R.M.A.)

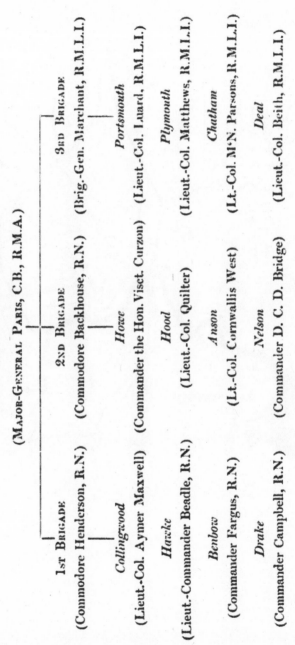

1st Brigade (Commodore Henderson, R.N.)	2nd Brigade (Commodore Backhouse, R.N.)	3rd Brigade (Brig.-Gen. Marchant, R.M.L.I.)
Collingwood (Lieut.-Col. Aymer Maxwell)	*Howe* (Commander the Hon. Visct Curzon)	*Portsmouth* (Lieut.-Col. Luard, R.M.L.I.)
Hawke (Lieut.-Commander Beadle, R.N.)	*Hood* (Lieut.-Col. Quilter)	*Plymouth* (Lieut.-Col. Matthews, R.M.L.I.)
Benbow (Commander Fargus, R.N.)	*Anson* (Lt.-Col. Cornwallis West)	*Chatham* (Lt.-Col. McN. Parsons, R.M.L.I.)
Drake (Commander Campbell, R.N.)	*Nelson* (Commander D. C. D. Bridge)	*Deal* (Lieut.-Col. Beith, R.M.L.I.)

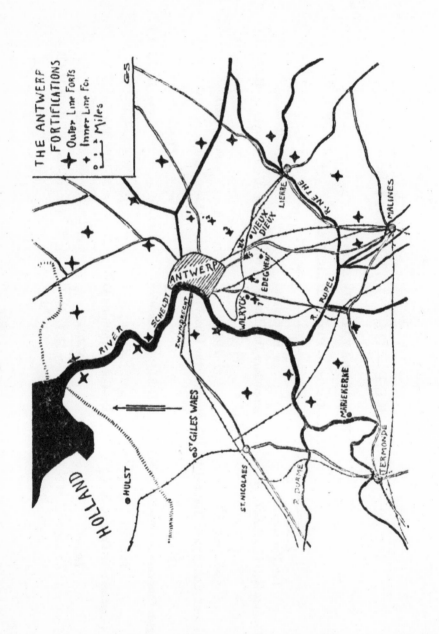

Chapter 2

The Antwerp Expedition
(October 4th-8th, 1914)

Lumber not thyself with many possessions, brevity is the soul of Kit.
Mudhook.

Being awakened at such an unreasonable hour on a cold winter's morning, it seemed probable that every minute was of the most vital importance, but yet it was well after 1 p.m. when we marched out of camp and entrained for Dover. The greater part of the night was spent on the quay, and it was not until the early hours of the following morning that we embarked in two cross-channel steamers and finally set sail, full of the joys of participating at last in the 'great adventure.' The submarine menace was at that time, of course, a very present evil and so, escorted by destroyers, we zigzagged in the orthodox manner to Dunkirk and arrived there without incident. The only item of interest during the voyage was an optimistic paymaster who sympathetically inquired the names of our next of kin and whether we had made a last will and testament, which he assured us was the correct method of procedure when embarking on such hazardous expeditions.

Dunkirk appeared to be a dull little town, and my only pleasant recollection of it is the welcome we received from the inhabitants and the sumptuous lunch they provided for us. Our arrival appeared to have an almost magical effect upon the Belgians, soldiers and civilians alike. Cheering crowds followed us everywhere. We were looked upon as the advance party of a great British army which was to drive the hated Germans from the country, and the naval armoured train was hailed as the precursor of artillery which would place the Belgians on a footing of equality with the enemy. A few hours were spent here serving out greatcoats and other necessaries, and that evening the first train started for the front.

Its complement consisted of details from various battalions, a few executive officers and myself—forming an advance party to test the line in case it might have been cut. My travelling companions were three officers and an enormous Cheshire cheese—the latter hastily pushed into the compartment by our efficient quartermaster. We stopped at various stations, and at each were welcomed by the local inhabitants, who cheered us uproariously and supplied us with abundant water to drink, but, as one of my fellow travellers, a Highlander, remarked, forgot the wherewithal to add to it, and so our Scotch friend had to depend on the contents of his own well-filled flask. For solid food we had—the cheese.

On arriving at Antwerp we learned that a large German patrol had been seen, apparently intent on cutting the line. They appeared to have been unsuccessful, however, as troops were still able to come through until October 6th.

On October 4th, the Royal Marine Brigade arrived at Edeghen and occupied trenches facing Lierre, with outposts on the River Nethe. They relieved the 21st Belgian Regiment, which was quite worn out with the hardships of the preceding days. On October 6th, the two naval brigades detrained at Wilryck, a small village close to Antwerp City, and occupied trenches between Forts 2 and 7. The circle of outer forts had already been pierced, and now, under cover of a heavy barrage, the enemy crossed the river. The Belgian chasseurs made a gallant though unsuccessful counter-attack, and it was soon obvious that our position was untenable. The Royal Marines were then ordered to retire to the inner line of forts which the naval brigades were occupying.

Our artillery, at this time, consisted of a number of field guns left behind by the Belgians, a few naval guns, and an armoured train of four 4.7 guns in charge of Lieutenant-Commander Littlejohn, R.N.— totally inadequate, of course, against the Austro-German siege train of 6, 8, 11, and 15-inch howitzers, fresh from the reduction of Liège and Namur. Howitzers of such calibre, commoner now than then, have gone to prove that few positions are impregnable, given suitable and adequate artillery. Whereas the German guns had an effective range of eight miles, that of the Belgian artillery was only five. My own battalion occupied a position between Forts 6 and 7, and the intervals between the other forts were likewise held by other units of the division.

26

The large numbers of Belgian troops we met on our way up to the trenches assured us that things were going well—an opinion quite in contrast with that of a Marine whose opinion was 'it's 'ot, Sir, 'ellish 'ot'—a description which I later entirely agreed with.

My impression of these trenches, the first I had ever seen, was distinctly discouraging. They were shallow and broad, and instead of being dug in, were mainly built up. Where the fire-step should have been were primitive dugouts which afforded neither comfort nor safety. In front of the trenches was an elaborate system of electrified barbed wire on which our searchlights played incessantly. Roofing over us was an artificial network of branches and foliage—a mode of camouflage, it struck me at the time, on a par with the ostrich who buries his head in the sand and hopes to pass as a palm-tree. Battalion headquarters was a small unpretentious stone erection which might possibly have kept out a summer shower, but was totally unfitted to with-stand even the lightest artillery. There was no sign of any support or reserve lines.

On arrival, the battalion at once commenced to deepen and improve generally the trenches, whilst I attempted to make arrangements for evacuation of wounded. This was somewhat complicated by the fact that my stretcher-bearers, who had merely been selected at random from the fighting personnel of the battalion, were all anxious to rejoin their comrades in the firing line.

It was extraordinarily difficult to find a suitable aid post. There were one or two buildings within a short distance of the trenches, but many were still occupied by their owners, who were quite unprepared for a sudden evacuation and could not believe that such a course was ever likely to be necessary. One building, which appeared to be of the nature of a monastic infirmary, seemed to be suitable for my purpose, and so was commandeered as a field hospital. It was truly a most affecting sight to see the good people moving their patients and household goods along the road to safety. Some were able to walk, many had been bedridden for years and had to be carried, whilst a few were conveyed in rough carts which jolted them terribly.

On returning to the trenches, I was somewhat disconcerted to find no trace of my battalion, but eventually I ran them to ground in their new position between Forts 3 and 4, where they were busily employed improving the very primitive trenches in that situation. All night long a hail of shells passed over our heads into doomed Antwerp. Fires soon broke out in the city and, as the water supply had been cut off, no attempt could be made to subdue them. A bombardment of

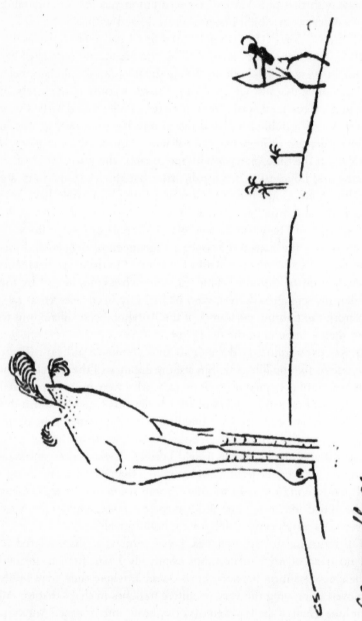

Camouflage.

increasing intensity was also opened on all the trenches, gun positions, and roads, making our position far from enviable. Amongst the killed was Lieutenant-Colonel Aymer Maxwell, a most popular and gallant officer, who was doing magnificent work in superintending the digging of our trenches. The evacuation of wounded was an exceedingly difficult problem, as there were no certain means of transport to Antwerp and no place of safety on arriving there.

By October 7th, the desperate plight of the city was obvious to all. It was evident that we could hold the enemy in check no longer and that reinforcements were not forthcoming. Hence in the evening, the Belgian government left the city, the ships lying in the docks were destroyed, and the great oil reservoirs were set on fire. On the following day official proclamations were posted up, advising the inhabitants to leave the city without delay, and a general exodus both by land and sea commenced.

It was now quite clear that to save the Naval Division from annihilation we must retire, and this was commenced on the evening of October 8th. It was a much more difficult operation than would appear, as all the roads were crowded with refugees, vehicles of every kind, and large herds of cattle. Most of the refugees in their hasty flight forgot to provide themselves with provisions, and many, worn out by fatigue and lack of food, were unable to continue the journey. Expectant mothers gave birth to premature children and the aged died of exposure. The confusion was indescribable and the noise deafening, as the weary, starving, homeless, hopeless Belgians shuffled along, the cries of the women and children drowned by the hum of motors, the rattle of carts, the clattering of hoofs, the groans of the wounded, the alternate pleading and cursing of the men, and the roar of guns in the near distance.

As far as I personally was concerned, I had not the slightest idea where we were going or what we were to do when we got to our destination. In the black darkness we trudged through cross country lanes, leaving behind the dull glare of the burning city. After what seemed an interminable march, we entrained at St. Giles Waes and finally reached England on October 10th.

Of the remainder of the division, the Royal Marine and 2nd Brigades eventually reached Bruges and Ostend by all conceivable routes, but a large proportion of three battalions of the 1st Brigade, owing to some as yet unexplained reason, went into Holland, where they were interned. The last train which attempted to get through was crowded with refugees, and great difficulty was experienced in finding accommodation for the troops. It was finally held up and derailed at St. Nicholaes by a strong German patrol. The scene which followed was indescribable. Women and children screaming with terror greatly hampered a successful resistance, and to all appearances our troops were entirely surrounded. The occupants of the train were ordered by a German officer to surrender. 'Surrender be damned; Royal Marines never surrender,' cried Major Arthur French, and collecting his men, took up a position on the railway track, covered the retirement of the remainder of the party, and finally, calling on his men, they cut their way through to safety—altogether an episode entirely in keeping with the fine traditions of the Royal Marine Corps.

The reasons of this expedition seem to require some explanation, and in order that the reader may appreciate the '*whys and wherefores,*' brief mention must be made of the circumstances which led up to the Naval Division being sent to Antwerp at all.

Towards the end of September 1914, the Belgian army assumed the offensive, and it seemed possible that they might recapture Brussels. In order to prevent this, von Böhm massed the greater proportion of his army in Belgium, with the object of stemming the advance and also of gaining possession of Antwerp. This city, with its double ring of forts, only just completed before the outbreak of war, was naturally considered by the Allies to be almost impregnable. The reason it was not so can possibly be explained by the fact that the majority of its guns and defences had been manufactured by Germany and the town itself contained 50,000 Germans, many of whom held high municipal and civil posts. On the other hand, it may have been due to our lack of appreciation of the terribly destructive effects of modern heavy artillery.

The unexpected news that the forts were being rapidly demolished, made it a certainty that the city must soon be captured, and Mr. Churchill, after a personal inspection of the defences, decided to send over the R.N.D. to hold the Germans in check until reinforcements could arrive from the allied armies in France.

The idea certainly appeared sound, but military critics are unanimous that, to carry out such a scheme, a very much larger force, with adequate artillery, was quite essential, and that the attempt with such a small force was poor strategy. The Admiralty at a later date published the reasons why the Royal Naval Division was selected for this venture:

Because the need for them was urgent and bitter; because mobile troops could not be spared for fortress duties; because they were the nearest and could be embarked the quickest; and because their training, though incomplete, was as far advanced as that of a large portion, not only of the forces defending Antwerp, but of the enemy force attacking. The Naval Division was sent to Antwerp, not as an isolated incident, but as part of a large operation for the relief of the city. Other and more powerful considerations prevented this from being carried through.

The results attained by the Antwerp Expedition are best described by quoting Field Marshal Sir John French's dispatch of December 5th, 1914.

In forwarding this report to the Army Council at the request of the Lords Commissioners of the Admiralty, I have to state that, from a comprehensive review of all the circumstances, the force of Marines and Naval Brigades which assisted in the defence of Antwerp was handled by General Paris with great skill and boldness. Although the results did not include the actual saving of the fortress, the action of the force under General Paris certainly delayed the enemy for a considerable time, and assisted the Belgian army to be withdrawn in a condition to enable it to reorganise and refit, and regain its value as a fighting force. The destruction of war material and ammunition—which, but for the intervention of this force, would have proved of great value to the enemy—was thus able to be carried out. The assistance which the Belgian army has rendered throughout the subsequent course of the operations on the Canal and Yser River has been a valuable asset to the allied cause, and such help must be regarded as an outcome of the intervention of General Paris's force. I am further of opinion that the moral effect produced on the minds of the Belgian army by this necessarily desperate attempt to bring them succour before it was too late, has been of great value to their use and efficiency as a fighting force.

Our total casualties, including missing, were 2627, and though no other division so ill-equipped and so inadequately trained would have done any better, it made people look upon the R.N.D. with an amused tolerance which they scarcely attempted to conceal.

The survivors of the expedition eventually reached England—the majority by more or less official routes, but some after many adventures returned home in most extraordinary disguises. I well remember Lieutenant West of the Hawke Battalion who was shipped across in what I take to have been a plumber's outfit—at any rate he carried a piece of lead piping in his hand.

On arrival in England, the division concentrated in its original camps, but early in 1915 it was moved *en masse* to Blandford—a sleepy country town in Dorset. My few recollections of this place are associated with constant rain, thick mud and draughty, uncomfortable huts. The camp was situated on the Downs around the old racecourse, some miles distant from the village. Here we spent a few weeks busily training for our next 'great adventure.'

RETURNING FROM ANTWERP

BLANDFORD

CHAPTER 3

Eastward Bound, Lemnos and Port Said

We who pursue
Our business with unslacking stride.
Traverse in troops, with care-filled breast,
The soft Mediterranean side.
The Nile, the East.
  Matthew Arnold.

On the night of February 28th, 1915, the Royal Naval Division sailed from Avonmouth and, after a pleasant, though uneventful voyage, arrived at Malta. Valetta, the capital of the island, is a town of great historical interest, but to the casual visitor is chiefly noted for its fine opera-house, its luxurious club, and the very moderate prices charged by the shopkeepers for both the necessities and luxuries of life. We had a most amusing time ashore, first doing a little shopping, and finally ending up with dinner at the club and a visit to the Alhambra, that celebrated variety theatre so popular amongst the junior officers of the Service. As there had been no time to lay in a stock of tropical kit before leaving England, many of us invested in 'reach me down' khaki drill uniforms. These curious, ill-fitting garments were later productive of much mirth. One of my professional brethren appeared in his for the first time at Port Said—'No pierrots on this part of the beach' was the cry as he blushingly perambulated the shore, and such was his innate modesty that he did not wear them again until Gallipoli was reached, where it scarcely mattered what you wore provided you kept cool.

After leaving Malta, our course lay past some of the Greek islands.

They looked beautiful in the clear southern atmosphere across the intervening belt of bright blue sea, but we had yet to discover that the best and only comfortable way of seeing them is from a ship. Stay aboard, that's my advice—it prevents disappointment. Personally I was lucky enough to be in the *Franconia*, and thoroughly enjoyed the voyage; there was plenty of work, any amount of amusements, and no food restrictions. The mornings were chiefly spent on parade, seeing the sick, vaccinating, lecturing on elementary first aid, and being taught the mysteries of 'submarine' drill; the afternoons were filled in with sports on deck and the evenings with concerts or bridge. In fact, as one of my west country friends remarked, 'it was a *proper* tour.'

On the cold, windy evening of March 12th we reached Lemnos, and found Mudros Harbour looking about the dreariest place imaginable. In every direction were low, desolate shores with high, bleak mountains in the background; here and there were a few red-roofed cottages, but these were the only signs of life ashore. The actual bay, however, presented a somewhat more lively spectacle. It was crowded with a multitude of ships of every description—battleships, cruisers, troopships, storeships, minesweepers, and submarines. After landing we soon came across some of the Plymouth Marines who had taken part in the operations of March 4th at Kum Kale and Sedd-el-Bahr. A half company had been landed at each of these points. The Sedd-el-Bahr guns having been temporarily silenced by the Fleet, the Royal Marines on this side of the straits advanced some distance inland without serious opposition, and withdrew again with few casualties.

The party on the Kum Kale side, however, met with a very determined resistance and sustained about forty casualties, chiefly due to machine-gun fire from windmills commanding the beach, and had not the ships opened a heavy bombardment, few would have returned from this landing. It is not generally known that even these were not the first landings in the Dardanelles. As early as February parties of Royal Marines, disembarked from ships, had marched through Krithia and reached Achi Baba with little or no opposition, whilst other detachments had gone ashore at Kum Kale in a like peaceful manner. In view of subsequent events, it seems strange that the ground could not have been permanently occupied then, instead of waiting until April 25th, by which time the Turks, now fully alive to our designs, had strongly fortified the position. This long delay has been blamed for the failure of the campaign, but it must be remembered that the change of plans consequent on our failure to force the Narrows on

March 14th naturally meant delay—more troops had to be sent from home, and even when these arrived the weather was unfavourable for landing operations.

The original plan of campaign appears to have been for the Naval Division to supply demolition parties, and occupy the forts after their reduction by the ships' guns. What prevented the carrying out of this scheme was the fact that the naval attempt to force the Narrows on March 14th failed disastrously. In this very gallant, though unsuccessful venture, six ships were put out of action—*Bouvet, Ocean,* and *Irresistible* were sunk, and *Suffren, Gaulois,* and *Inflexible* badly damaged. *Bouvet* sank in three minutes and only twenty-five of her crew were saved, whilst *Ocean,* taking longer to sink, only lost two men. *Irresistible* was mined, and had thirty of her ship's company killed or wounded, and *Suffren,* also mined, had one turret entirely blown away. *Gaulois* was so damaged by shell-fire that she had to be beached on Rabbit Island, and *Inflexible,* striking a mine, was with great difficulty taken to Tenedos. Though altogether a most heroic action, and deserving of much greater success, its failure quite negatived any hope of further efforts in this direction, and at last the fact was recognised by all that a large landing force was necessary to co-operate with the Fleet.

Mr. Granville Fortescue, who was with the Turks at this time, gives a very clear account of the action from a Turkish point of view in his book, *Russia, the Balkans, and the Dardanelles.* Apparently our shooting was excellent, but the damage to the guns in the forts was comparatively small. According to the commander of one of these, thirty-three shells fell in the traverse and seventy-six in the gorge of the fort, but by sheer ill-luck only one struck in an embrasure. He also says that the shells of the *Queen Elizabeth* broke into only ten fragments and so did not do so much damage as was expected. Mr. Fortescue was with the Turkish army at the time and had ample opportunity of conversing with German and Turkish officers, and his book, published in September 1915, gives a clear idea of the Dardanelles situation, and one contrasting strongly with the spirit of exaggerated optimism that prevailed in the press for the first months of the campaign.

During this period the Royal Naval Division was in camp at Lemnos, and we had ample opportunity of studying the island and its inhabitants. Lemnos is a mountainous volcanic island enclosing Mudros Harbour, around which are grouped the villages of Mudros, Sarpi, and Portianos. The chain of mountains on the south-west of the harbour entrance is chiefly noteworthy on account of the names of its highest

MUDROS HARBOUR

MUDROS BAY AND SARPI

peaks—Yam, Sylloc, Eb and Denmad, which on reading each word backwards becomes 'May Collys be damned.' I do not know Collys, but it seems a pretty sentiment and has immortalised his name long after he himself is forgotten. Castro, the capital of Lemnos, is situated on the other side of the island from the bay and is of considerable historic interest. Its houses lie along the shore of a small inlet of the sea, and it is flanked by a tall rock on which stands a fine old Norman castle. Its shops are poor, and though a good dinner can be obtained at the Hôtel de France, those who spend a night there are apt to have their repose somewhat disturbed by small insects the size of which is no criterion of the amount of irritation they cause.

Not many miles from Castro is the village of Thermos. It is a small hamlet which, as its name implies, has a natural spring of exceedingly hot water and a very well-appointed marble bath largely used in times of peace by the upper-class Greeks, both as a prophylactic and as a cure for nearly every disease to which flesh is heir. It was very greatly patronised by the troops. The houses in the island are mean, dirty hovels, though picturesque enough in the distance, and are inhabited by primitive, ignorant peasants who apparently were never so wealthy in their lives as during our occupation. Their mode of conducting business was mainly one of extortion, and they rarely kept anything in their shops which was at all worth having. One of their hobbies was an illicit traffic in inferior wines and spirits, and hence it was the duty of our A.P.Ms, to discover them *in flagrante delicto* and hand them over to the civil authorities for punishment, which, as a rule, took the form of a large fine and transportation to the mainland of Greece. A little of their liquor went a long way, and not infrequently I was called upon in my professional capacity to treat men who were exceedingly sorry they had ever been persuaded to partake of such noxious beverages.

These island dwellers were in the habit of overloading their unfortunate animals to an incredible extent. It was no uncommon sight to see a small pony carrying not only a stout peasant and his buxom spouse, but also in addition an enormous sack of grain. There can be no doubt but that in England we lay too much stress on the importance of a large horse for weight-carrying purposes, whereas many a much smaller animal is capable of greater work and endurance, yet certainly the Greek farmer goes to the opposite extreme. On the whole, he is an unattractive personage—some say the cut of his trousers has a demoralising influence on his character, and perhaps they are right.

Before the last Balkan War, Lemnos belonged to Turkey and was

A Stout Peasant and
his Buxom Spouse

The Primitive
Peasant of Mudros

Graeco-Roman Wrestling

Cairo and the Pyramids

never definitely handed over to the Greeks. Hence as the ownership of the island was *sub judice*, we seized the opportunity of annexing it, and decided to utilise it as an inter-base headquarters for the Dardanelles operations, in spite of the fact that it was sixty miles from Gallipoli and, having no suitable store-houses, all material had to be loaded from one ship to another. Before the peninsula was evacuated, however, everything had changed—busy wharves, camps, hospitals, supply dumps, and canteens had sprung up everywhere, and General Headquarters was luxuriously housed at Portianos and in the *Aragon*, a very celebrated ship which was popularly believed to be aground on empty champagne bottles.

Shortly after our arrival, the commander-in-chief, accompanied by his divisional generals and their staffs, embarked on H.M.S. *Phaeton*, and set out to reconnoitre the intended landing places in Gallipoli. This seemed to indicate the speedy onset of active operations, and hence it came as somewhat of a surprise when on March 24th the R.N.D. was ordered to Port Said and the 29th Division to Alexandria. This course was adopted in order to restow the military stores and equipment, and rearrange the troops in a manner more suitable for quick disembarkation. Many units had arrived from England with their baggage in one ship and themselves in another and hence numerous articles were missing. One transport sergeant of my acquaintance reporting on the horses to his commanding officer ingenuously stated, 'Took twenty-eight aboard, Sir, one died, and I've got twenty-nine off.'

On arrival at Port Said, two brigades went into camp on the sands near the golf-course, whilst the 2nd Brigade was sent to the Canal defences, where a short time previously the Turkish army had made the dramatic attempt to force the Canal in pontoons, which had only been frustrated by the gunfire of the Fleet.

We quickly settled down at Port Said to ordinary camp routine, and later began to re-embark our gear in readiness for the Gallipoli landing. The officer in charge of this operation caused us endless amusement. His methods of getting full value out of working parties were wonderful, and his manner of soliloquising for long periods in many languages without once repeating himself called forth our heartfelt admiration. The one drawback to our stay at Port Said was the great contrast between the food we were now given and that of the *Franconia* regime. We were now at the mercy of the battalion cooks, who were pure novices at the game. Many of them proved to themselves—and more particularly to us—that their capabilities lay in other directions, and hence not infrequently we dined in the town. Such expeditions always ended with a visit to a theatre or music-hall. These latter always provided an amusing, if none too skilled performance.

The *pièce de résistance* was usually a Graeco-Roman wrestling contest in which every bout consisted of fat, greasy, breathless men gripping one another in an endearing embrace and, when the opportunity arose, slapping the more prominent and fleshy parts of each other's anatomy—with shouts of laughter, to the intense joy of the *habitués*. At a word from the referee the combatants sprang apart and bowed to the plaudits of the multitude.

One bright incident of our stay was forty-eight hours' leave to Cairo, which was a revelation to those of us who had never been in Egypt before. The oriental, with his bright clothes, vivacious manner, picturesque language and ready wit is always a person of interest, if not of integrity. His conversation is voluble and interlarded with slang from all the countries bordering on the Mediterranean. He can also talk a kind of pidgin-English and occasionally can even write it. I remember one individual who had been in the habit of supplying an officers' mess in Alexandria, wrote a most amusing letter, when accused of charging too heavily for his goods. It ran as follows:—

Dear Sir the Captain—
Dear Sir,—I show you that the Colonel bade us yesterday bear the shop, because we are selling the things dear, but you may ask the cook if we sell dear or cheap. We give him the eggs like as in the market five eggs with two big *piastres*, and all the remaining things are very cheap, and as you said I can sell.
You know Sir when the goods are cheap, it is cheap for the men and seller, *vice versa*. And I know Sir that you like to help the poor man. Help me, because I am a poor man and I have big family.
At last I ask God to help you and lives in a good happy life.—
Your obedient servant,
Issa Ibrahim.

The 2nd Brigade, having spent a few days at Kantara in the Canal defences, rejoined us in time for an inspection by Sir Ian Hamilton, just prior to our departure. The day chosen for this review was grillingly hot, and as on all such occasions, we paraded early and had a long time to wait. The only incident to relieve the monotony was that one officer's horse went to sleep and deposited his likewise somnolent rider head first in the sand. Fortunately both my equestrian friend and his somewhat irate commanding officer had amicably settled their differences before the G.O.C. arrived, and the actual inspection went off exceedingly well.

In a few days' time we left Port Said, and on the morning of April 16th arrived at Skyros, which was the rendezvous for the transports carrying the Royal Naval Division. On the way there the s.s. *Manitou* was attacked by a Turkish torpedo boat and had a very exciting time. The skipper, who was a German, allowed ten minutes to get into the boats—a most unusual concession from one of his nationality—and then fired two torpedoes at the ship. Fortunately both of them missed, and our destroyers, in answer to the S.O.S. signal, were quickly on the scene. The enemy went off at full speed and was chased away to the Island of Kios, where she ran aground.

At Skyros the routine was very similar to that at Lemnos and consisted mainly in practising landing operations. The island itself is on the whole rather duller and more uninteresting than Lemnos, and its chief inhabitant is the tortoise, whose phlegmatic temperament can, of course, stand anything. We stayed here longer than was primarily intended, as the high winds prevailing at the time precluded any possibility of landing in Gallipoli, but at last, on April 24th, our fleet of ten transports, two supply ships, and a hospital ship in three lines ahead sailed out of harbour, led by H.M.S. *Canopus, Kennet*, and *Dartmouth*. That evening we passed Mount Athos rising out of the deep blue of a calm sea and sharply outlined against the red glow of the setting sun—a gorgeous spectacle never to be forgotten.

On the following morning, the ships sailed up the Gulf of Saros, and while the men-of-war bombarded various points in the vicinity of Bulair, the transports dropped anchor midway between the north and south shores. In the evening a tow of eight boats, each carrying twenty men, made for the north shore, keeping the Island of Microsaros well to the east. This demonstration was merely a feint to attract attention, and during its progress Lieutenant Freyberg, R.N.V.R., swam ashore, lit flares on the beach, reconnoitred the position, and, I believe, discovered the situation of a Turkish division. This was the first opportunity he had of showing that great initiative and wonderful personal gallantry, which at a later date gained him the V.C. at Beaucourt-sur-Ancre.

It seems rather doubtful whether we really deceived the Turks or

MOUNT ATHOS

not; our gunfire was of such a desultory character that it appears we would have been much better employed at one of the principal landing-places where the main army was getting a reception greatly in contrast with that of February, when parties went ashore with little opposition.

All sorts of criticisms have been levelled at the conduct of the campaign, especially with reference to the sites chosen for landing. 'Why not have landed at Bulair or Eanos or on both sides of the entrance?' asks the armchair critic. In answer I would argue that, in order to help the Navy to force the Straits, some piece of land in direct relation to them had to be seized, and hence Eanos was unsuitable. Bulair, of course, seems a more likely place, as the peninsula is only 3½ miles broad at this point, and by pushing a well-equipped force across here, a large part of the Turkish army would be cut off. On the other hand, there are two objections: firstly, the water at the only available landing-place is very shallow and the adjacent land marshy and unsuitable; secondly, a very large force would have been required, owing to exposure of both its flanks and to the fact that it would be under the direct observation of the Bulair lines, one of the most strongly fortified positions of Gallipoli.

As regards landing on both sides of the Straits, this was done, but it was found impossible to continue the operations on the southern shore without imperilling the success of the Gallipoli Campaign, and hence the troops were withdrawn from Kum Kale. Had it not been for shortage of men and guns, there can be no doubt that it would have been better to occupy both sides, and so save the Gallipoli army from that endless scourge, enfilade shelling from the Asiatic shore.

To understand the difficulties of the campaign, a map of the Dardanelles must be studied, Gallipoli is a peninsula 53 miles long by 3 to 12 miles broad, bounded to the north-west by the Gulf of Saros, and to the south-east by the Dardanelles and the Sea of Marmora. Its shores consist of cliffs rising to a height of 100 to 200 feet with few sandy beaches; its interior is fissured by deep gullies, and the water supply is scanty in many places and there are no deep wells. The country, as a whole, is very hilly, and though few of the hills attain any great size, they command every inch of the undulating plains beneath them.

In addition, the weather has to be taken into consideration. On the whole it is a very constant quantity, and the changes of the seasons take place with remarkable precision. Spring occurs early and soon gives place to a very hot season, and the weather remains fine with hardly

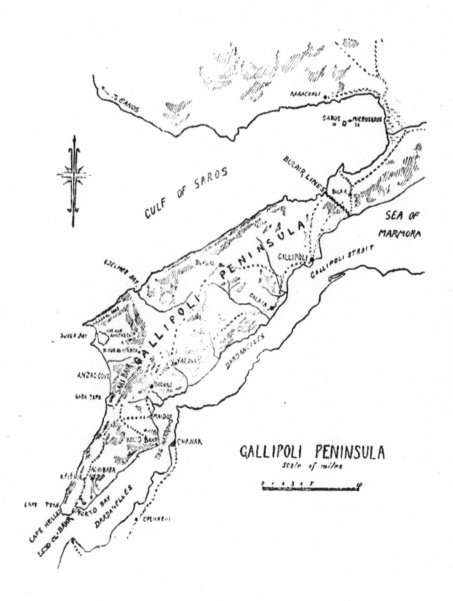

GALLIPOLI PENINSULA
scale of miles

a break until October, when it becomes somewhat unsettled and the temperature drops, accompanied by high winds. These gales usually last about three days and vary greatly in direction, but as a general rule, there is not much rain until January, though occasionally a cold snap accompanied by a heavy storm sets in before the end of the year.

THE GALLIPOLI LANDING—APRIL 1915

ROYAL NAVAL DIVISION

(Major-General Paris, C.B., R.M.A.)

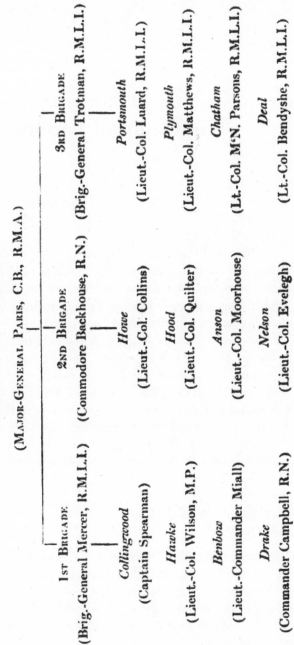

1st Brigade
(Brig.-General Mercer, R.M.L.I.)

Collingwood
(Captain Spearman)

Hawke
(Lieut.-Col. Wilson, M.P.)

Benbow
(Lieut.-Commander Miall)

Drake
(Commander Campbell, R.N.)

2nd Brigade
(Commodore Backhouse, R.N.)

Howe
(Lieut.-Col. Collins)

Hood
(Lieut.-Col. Quilter)

Anson
(Lieut.-Col. Moorhouse)

Nelson
(Lieut.-Col. Evelegh)

3rd Brigade
(Brig.-General Trotman, R.M.L.I.)

Portsmouth
(Lieut.-Col. Luard, R.M.L.I.)

Plymouth
(Lieut.-Col. Matthews, R.M.L.I.)

Chatham
(Lt.-Col. M'N. Parsons, R.M.L.I.)

Deal
(Lt.-Col. Bendyshe, R.M.L.I.)

CHAPTER 4

The Gallipoli Landing

General Headquarters,
21st April 1915.

Force Order (Special).

Soldiers of France and of the King!

Before us lies an adventure unprecedented in modern war. Together with our comrades of the Fleet, we are about to force a landing upon an open beach in face of positions which have been vaunted by our enemies as impregnable.

The landing will be made good by the help of God and the Navy: the position will be stormed, and the war brought one step nearer to a glorious close.

'Remember,' said Lord Kitchener, when bidding *adieu* to your Commander, 'Remember, once you set foot in the Gallipoli Peninsula, you must fight the thing through to a finish.'

The whole world will be watching our progress. Let us prove ourselves worthy of the great feat of arms entrusted to us.

Ian Hamilton, General.

Printing Section,
Med. Exped. Force,
G.H.Q.

Whether rightly or wrongly, Sir Ian Hamilton decided to make two main attacks—one at Cape Helles and one at Gaba Tepe. The covering force for the former consisted of the 29th Division and two battalions of the Royal Naval Division, whilst the Australians, New Zealanders, and four battalions of the Royal Naval Division were engaged in the latter venture.

On the morning of April 25th, 1915, the attack on Cape Helles

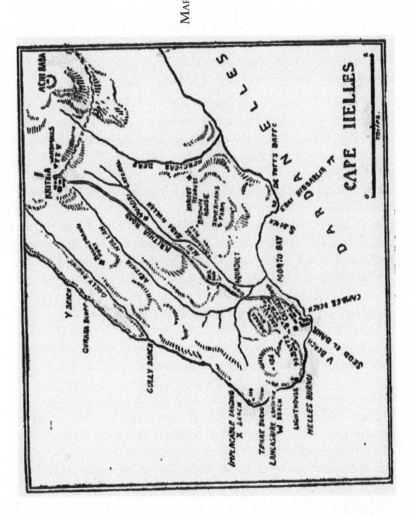

was launched at six points simultaneously, and was aided by gunfire from H.M.S. *Swiftsure, Implacable, Cornwallis, Albion, Vengeance, Lord Nelson, Prince George, Euryalus, Talbot, Minerva*, and *Dublin*. The landing near Gaba Tepe was accomplished on the same day, with the assistance of the battleships *Queen, London, Prince of Wales, Triumph*, and *Majestic*, the cruiser *Bacchante*, the destroyers *Beagle, Bulldog, Foxhound, Scourge, Colne, Uske, Chelmer*, and *Ribble*, the balloon-ship *Hector*, and fifteen trawlers.

For purposes of description it is best to describe each landing separately.

'*S*' *Beach.*—The 2nd South Wales Borderers and a portion of the Anson Battalion landed at Morto Bay, and taking up a position near De Tott's battery, maintained themselves there with comparatively few casualties until they were reinforced on April 27th.

'*V*' *Beach.*—This is a narrow strip of sand stretching from Sedd-el-Bahr Castle to Cape Helles and bounded by a bank about six feet in height, beyond which the ground gently rises towards the village on the one hand and the cliff of Cape Helles on the other. It was admirably suited for defence, and the enemy had taken full advantage of the natural lie of the ground. Sedd-el-Bahr village, though very severely handled by our ships, still afforded great protection for Turkish machine-guns and snipers, and every house had been converted into a miniature fort. The Dublin Fusiliers, Munster Fusiliers, Hampshires, the West Riding Field Company of Engineers, and a party of the Anson Battalion were detailed for this landing. Under a terrific bombardment, the collier *River Clyde* was run ashore and a bridge of lighters swept into position, forming a gangway to the beach.

The task of connecting up these lighters was one of great difficulty and danger, and it was entirely due to the superb gallantry of Commander Unwin, R.N., that it was ever accomplished. Troops then poured out of holes cut in the side of the ship and made for the shore under a veritable hail of shot and shell which well-nigh annihilated the heroic band. Finally a handful of men reached the shelter of the low bank on the foreshore and maintained their position in the face of overwhelming odds. Of the wounded, many fell into the water, and dragged down by their heavy equipment, were drowned, whilst others, in spite of most gallant attempts to rescue them, were again wounded or killed.

The enemy, taking full advantage of the natural strength of his po-

'V' Beach and s.s. 'River Clyde'

S.S. River Clyde

By Lieutenant Wace, R.N.
and G. Sparrow

sition, was able to prevent the landing being continued on this beach, and the plight of our men became so serious that the attempt was almost abandoned, and indeed some of the troops destined for this attack were diverted to 'W' Beach. However, under cover of darkness more troops were landed to reinforce the heroic little party, and together they advanced on Sedd-el-Bahr Castle, but in spite of their gallant efforts they were driven back to the beach by sheer force of numbers, and only saved from complete destruction by the timely intervention of the ships' guns. On the following day, under the magnificent leadership of Major Doughty-Wyllie, the castle was stormed.

The following official account of how Sub-Lieutenant Arthur Walderne St. Clair Tisdall, R.N.V.R., gained his Victoria Cross is illustrative of the good work done by a platoon of the Anson Battalion at this landing:

> During the landing from the s.s. *River Clyde* at 'V' Beach in the Gallipoli Peninsula, Sub-Lieutenant Tisdall, hearing wounded men on the beach calling for assistance, jumped into the water, and pushing a boat in front of him, went to their rescue. He was, however, obliged to obtain help, and took with him on two trips Leading Seaman Malia, and on other trips Chief Petty Officer Perring, and Leading Seamen Curtiss and Parkinson. In all, Sub-Lieutenant Tisdall made four or five trips between the ship and the shore, and was thus responsible for rescuing several wounded men under heavy and accurate fire.

Camber.—This is a piece of dead ground just east of Sedd-el-Bahr, where a half company of the Dublin Fusiliers were landed, but being unable to advance they were soon withdrawn.

'*W' Beach.*—Lancashire Landing, as this beach was called later, is a strip of sand to the west of the castle, lying between the steep cliffs of Cape Helles on the south and Cape Tekke on the north. Our attack on this point was anticipated by the Turks, and every means taken to frustrate it. The rising ground was honeycombed with well-sited trenches, bristling with machine-guns, and barbed wire entanglements were everywhere, even under the water in the shallows. The Lancashire Fusiliers, with wonderful determination and courage, overcame all obstacles, and in spite of being repeatedly held up temporarily by uncut wire, which stretched in serried rows in every direction, joined forces with the Royal Fusiliers from 'X' Beach, and storming the redoubts on Hills 114 and 136, entrenched themselves in a line stretching from there to just east of the lighthouse.

'*X*' *Beach*.—This strip of sand, lying to the north of Cape Tekke, is approximately two hundred yards in length and lies beneath a low cliff. A tow of boats from H.M.S. *Implacable* landed the Royal Fusiliers and a party of the Anson Battalion at this point. The battleship, standing close inshore, kept up an exceedingly accurate fire and enabled our troops to advance and link up with the Lancashire Fusiliers on their right. This attack was exceedingly successful, and the mountings of one of the captured guns may now be seen in the R.N. Barracks at Devonport.

'*Y*' *Beach*.—This narrow landing-place, situated due west of Krithia, lies at the foot of steep scrub covered cliffs. So inaccessible did it appear that no attack was expected, and the Plymouth Battalion Royal Marines, along with the King's Own Scottish Borderers, were able to scale the cliffs with little opposition. A further advance was, however, impossible, and being unable to get in touch with the Fusiliers on their right, in face of repeated counter-attacks by an enemy frequently reinforced, they were compelled merely to dig themselves in on the summit of the cliffs. Not only were they outnumbered, but the configuration of the ground favoured the enemy in such a way that our ships' guns could not be brought to bear on him. It is hollowed out like a cup of which the lip is formed by the summit of the cliffs, and reinforcements could be rushed up from Krithia and massed in the hollow with comparative safety. After holding out with great stubbornness during the day and following night, it was evident that our men would have to withdraw. The re-embarkation was carried out after a gallant rear-guard action in which the Royal Marines took an exceedingly prominent part.

Kum Kale.—While these operations were in progress on Gallipoli, the French effected a landing at Kum Kale on the opposite side of the entrance to the straits. They were assisted by the French Fleet and the Russian ship *Askold*, popularly known, on account of her five funnels, as the 'packet o' woodbines.' As the enemy was in great force it was considered inadvisable to proceed with this operation, and the troops withdrew, with 500 prisoners, and were diverted to 'V' Beach on the evening of the 26th.

'*Z*' *Beach*.—The Australian landing was planned to take place just north of Gaba Tepe, but owing to some error the troops were disembarked well to the north of the point chosen. ' Z ' Beach is about a thousand yards long and is commanded by scrub-covered cliffs and rocky spurs separated by deep ravines. The Turks, anticipating an attack at Gaba Tepe, had concentrated their forces there and were unprepared for the landing at Anzac Cove, but as the boats came inshore, they hurriedly massed at this point to resist the invaders. The Australians proved to be irresistible, and rushing the beach, drove the enemy at the point of the bayonet helter-skelter up the hills. Their rapid advance was only checked by the impassable nature of the country, which allowed the Turks time to bring up vast reserves of men and guns. From the outset our troops were greatly harassed by the howitzers of Chanak Forts and the guns of hostile ships lying in the safety of the Dardanelles, but these were to a certain extent neutralised by the accurate shooting of H.M.S. *Queen Elizabeth.*

On April 28th, the Nelson and three Royal Marine battalions, under the command of Brigadier-Generals Mercer and Trotman, landed and bivouacked in Shrapnel Valley. Two companies of the Nelsons were attached to the 3rd Australian Infantry Division, and along with a battalion under Lieutenant-Colonel Monash, took part in an attack on 'Dead Man's Work.' This was a very costly operation, the Nelsons alone losing six officers and eighty men killed, in addition to numerous wounded.

The remainder of this naval brigade were also heavily engaged, and it was here that Lance-Corporal Parker of the Royal Marines gained his well-earned V.C. The following is the official account of his very gallant exploits:

> On the night of April 30-May 1, 1915, a message asking for ammunition, water, and medical stores was received from an isolated fire trench at Gaba Tepe. A party of non-commissioned officers and men were detailed to carry water and ammunition, and in response to a call for a volunteer from among the stretcher-bearers, Parker at once came forward; he had, during the previous three days, displayed conspicuous bravery and energy under fire whilst in charge of the battalion stretcher-bearers. Several men had already been killed in a previous attempt to bring assistance to the men holding the fire trench.
>
> To reach this trench it was necessary to traverse an area at least four hundred yards wide, which was completely exposed and swept by rifle fire. It was already daylight when the party emerged from shelter, and at once one of the men was wound-

ed. Parker organised a stretcher party and then, going on alone, succeeded in reaching the fire trench, all the water and ammunition carriers being either killed or wounded. After his arrival he rendered assistance to the wounded in the trench, displaying extreme courage and remaining cool and collected in very trying circumstances. The trench had finally to be evacuated, and Parker helped to remove and attend the wounded, though he himself was seriously wounded during the operation.

Another incident in this stage of the operations deserving of especial mention was how Lieutenants Alcock and Empson of the Royal Marines, with a band of sixty men, defended a small portion of trench against overwhelming odds. Lieutenant Empson was finally killed, and Lieutenant Alcock compelled to withdraw his men, having held the trench for four nights and three days without food or water, until his ammunition was reduced to fifteen rounds per man.

On May 5th General Mercer's Brigade, in conjunction with the 9th Australian Brigade, occupied Quinn's Post and other advanced positions which they held until ordered to leave for Cape Helles on May 14th.

Meanwhile, those of us who were still on board the transport had ample opportunity of watching the fighting at all the landing-places. The shelling on both sides was intense. I counted fifty shrapnel shells in a minute bursting over a small sector of our trenches, whilst on our side the *Queen Elizabeth* completely demolished Maidos, the principal Turkish military base for both the northern and southern zones. The tame poet of the *Natal Newsletter* somewhat aptly describes the doings of the celebrated 'Q. E.'

When she goes a walking out, there's consternation
Among the baggy-trousered Eastern swells.
For she's slinging Cupid's arrows
In the region of their narrows.
Is our busy little Lizzie, in the dizzy Dardanelles.

On one occasion a Turkish gun, complete with its complement of men and horses, was blown into the air, just as it was coming into action near Lala Baba. The direct fire of our ships upon troops massing in the open was as spectacular as it was destructive, but one of the finest sights I have ever seen was that of a Turkish aeroplane hit by a 12-inch projectile. The cap of the unfortunate aviator is reputed to have been salved by a trawler, but nothing else could be found.

By the night of April 26th, Sir Ian Hamilton had given the lie to the German boast that Gallipoli was impregnable; and however small our footing might be, it was none the less firmly held.

On April 27th, the Drake Battalion and 29th Division advanced from De Tott's Battery to a point two miles north of Cape Tekke, and on the following day again advanced their line over three hundred yards. The fighting was of a very obstinate kind, and there were numerous counter-attacks. Enemy snipers were particularly active. With their bodies covered in foliage and their faces even of a similar green colour, they lay, indistinguishable from the neighbouring trees and undergrowth, taking their daily toll of life.

During the following two days no further advance was made, owing to the exhaustion of both sides, and the time was spent landing ammunition, horses, guns, and men. Amongst these reinforcements were the Howe and Hood Battalions of the Royal Naval Division, Cox's Indian Brigade, and the French Corps *Expéditionnaire d'Orient.*

On the evening of May 1st, the Turks made a very strong counter-attack which came perilously near success. After an intense artillery preparation, they suddenly advanced and were in our front line before their designs were realised. In some places they were so successful that many of our gunners were firing at point-blank range, and in some cases the breech-blocks were even removed, preparatory to retreat. At first the full force of the attack was felt on the right of the 86th Brigade, where the situation was only saved by the wonderful gallantry of the 6th Royal Scots, but later the Senegalese were forced back on the left of the French line, until the resulting gap was bridged by a naval battalion and the Worcesters. Early on the following morning, the Allies counter-attacked, but owing to the French being held up, enfilade fire from the right flank forced us to evacuate our gains.

During the next two days the enemy made repeated unsuccessful counter-attacks, sustaining heavy casualties on each occasion.

From the landing on April 25th and during the subsequent operations up to May 4th, our casualties had been very severe. Exclusive of the French, they amounted to 177 officers and 1990 men killed, 412 officers and 7807 men wounded, and 13 officers and 3580 men missing. The Turkish losses were purely a matter of conjecture, but they must have been truly appalling.

To my mind the most wonderful part of the whole operation was that the same men who went through that dreadful ordeal of the landing not only held their positions in face of the most determined counter-attacks, but also actually even advanced their line in places and firmly consolidated it. The Turks fought with the utmost gallantry and stubbornness and attacked repeatedly in close formation, hoping to drive us into the sea by sheer weight of numbers, but everywhere they were repulsed with enormous slaughter.

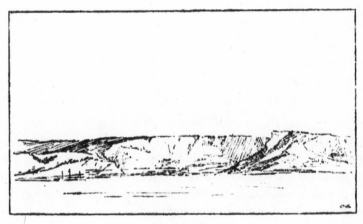

ANZAC COVE

CHAPTER 5

Subsequent Fighting and Life at Cape Helles

There is but one task for all,
For each one life to give.
Who stands if Freedom fall?
Who dies, if England live?
Kipling.

By May 4th the entire Naval Division was ashore, with the exception of parts of the field ambulances, including myself, and a few divisional details. We had had an excellent view of the landing, but it was now a weary, anxious time, as, owing to the configuration of the ground, much of the present fighting was out of sight, and all we could do was to watch the shells falling on Krithia village and wonder vaguely how our troops were faring. At last on May 6th, all doctors were disposed of, some to hospital ships or transports which had been commandeered for the reception of wounded, others to join their units ashore, whilst I was ordered to 'V' Beach to act as embarkation medical officer. Instructions were received to land mules, but to leave the wagons on board, an order productive of much discussion, only a few attributing it to the real cause—that there was neither occasion nor space for all our transport on the small foothold we then held.

Landing at 'W' Beach, my small party and I walked across Cape Helles, and finally arrived at 'V' Beach. The recent fighting had left its mark everywhere: crumbling trenches and torn, twisted barbed wire lay all around, great yawning shell-holes were on every hand, the lighthouse, smashed beyond all recognition, was merely a heap of fallen masonry and shattered glass, and the 9.2 guns of No. 1 Fort, hurled from their mountings, lay all bent and broken amongst the ruins of the stronghold.

In spite of the shelling, the scene was one of great activity. Dugouts, roads, gun positions, and horse lines were springing up everywhere; reinforcements, horses, artillery, and other equipment were being landed on the beaches, and primitive sandbag piers were in process of rapid construction. The Beach Master and Military Landing Officer of 'W' Beach were not only organising everything faultlessly, but also welcomed and refreshed all and sundry who drifted in the direction of their mess. The cordiality of their mutual relations was wonderful, considering how vague was the line of demarcation between naval and military control on the beaches.

Passing through the ruins of Sedd-el-Bahr village, 'V Beach, with the historic *River Clyde* and her bridge of lighters, came into view. Both the beach and the village were now under the control of the French, but all matters pertaining to embarkation and disembarkation were in the extraordinarily capable hands of Commander Unwin and his staff, who, by their wonderful skill and heroism, had rendered a landing at this spot possible.

Meanwhile hard fighting was still in progress, and from May 6th to 8th our line was advanced over six hundred yards. The troops engaged in this attack were the French, to whom was attached the 2nd R.N. Brigade, the 29th Division and a composite division, composed of a New Zealand Brigade, an Australian Brigade, and the Drake and Plymouth Battalions of the Royal Naval Division. The ground was extremely difficult to advance over and was well suited for defensive purposes. Gully Ravine and 'Seven Tree' Copse on the left, Kerevers Dere on the right, and a stronghold known as Zimmerman Farm greatly hampering our operations.

By May 8th, the losses in the Naval Division had been extremely heavy. Mr. Masefield in his book *Gallipoli* only mentions *one* battalion of the R.N.D. as being engaged in the April and May fighting. This is entirely erroneous, and in recognition of the fine work done by the 2nd (R.N.) Brigade, General d'Armade paraded them and officially thanked them for their splendid co-operation.

In the meantime it was not all peace on 'V' Beach. The French had installed many heavy guns amongst the ruins of Sedd-el-Bahr village, and these, in conjunction with a near-by battery of '75's,' kept up a lively bombardment to which the Turks replied by shelling us from the opposite shore with that famous gun known as 'Asiatic Annie.' The enemy's ammunition, however, was not as good as it might have been, and many of the shells which dropped on the beach were 'duds.' On one morning the *River Clyde* was hit 'full toss' six times in succession without the slightest damage being done. The *Dardanelles Driveller,* a journal published in the field and not unworthy of its name, alluded to these occurrences in its so-called advertisement column:

Amphi-Theatre Royal, V Beach
Twice Daily
A screaming farce entitled *Annie from Asia.*

Unfortunately this was a jest which very soon became no longer applicable, as the Turks obtained fresh supplies and treated us to an exhibition of their powers which was anything but a farce, scream-ing or otherwise. The French quite shared our respect for Annie, and posted a sentry on a haystack overlooking the Straits with instructions to blow a horn as soon as he saw a flash from the opposite shore. This gave us twenty seconds to take to ground, whilst the sentry occupied the interval in slipping down a hole in the interior of his haystack, in the hope that the hay would ward off any splinters coming in his direction.

After spending a few days at 'V' Beach, I received orders to join my unit which was encamped in Orchard Valley, a charming spot, with luxuriant olive-trees and gorgeous flowers, lying between the Krithia Road and Drake's Hill. Meanwhile the 42nd (Lancashire Territorial) Division had landed, and the line was held from left to right by Cox's Indian Brigade, 29th Division, 42nd Division, Royal Naval Division, and the French Corps *Expéditionnaire d'Orient.*

On May 12th Gurkha Bluff was taken, and on the night of May 26th the Royal Marines advanced over two hundred yards in the right centre sector near Achi Baba Nullah, but with the exception of these minor operations nothing occurred until June 4th. This delay has been criticised *ad nauseam* by all and sundry, and so I shall merely content myself with pointing out that, as both sides were exhausted with fight-ing, a temporary cessation of hostilities was the natural consequence, and as neither side had the preponderance of men necessary to carry on an offensive, trench warfare was inevitable.

Owing to the sinking of the *Goliath* on May 18th, the *Triumph* on May 25th, and the *Majestic* on May 27th, our transports were ordered to return to the Islands and G.H.Q. established itself at Imbros. As a result of these misadventures, Turkish aeroplanes dropped a number of

GUNS OF No. 1 FORT

BROWN HOUSE

proclamations over our lines, and the accompanying document, which fell in our field ambulance, is a fair example. It is signed, with a prophetic insight, that is so essentially Turkish, by the officer commanding the Turkish forces near Sedd-el-Bahr. But throughout its length the hand of the heavy German, so devoid of humour, is perfectly obvious. As an example of serio-comic literature it is possibly unique!

PROCLAMATION TO THE ANGLO-FRENCH EXPEDITIONARY FORCES

Protected by a heavy fire from a powerful Fleet, you had been able to land on the Gallipoli Peninsula on and since April 25th.

Backed up by those same men-of-war you could establish yourselves at two points of the Peninsula.

All your endeavours to advance into the inner parts of the Peninsula have come to failure under your heavy losses although your ships have done their utmost to assist you by a tremendous cannonade implying an enormous waste of ammunition.

Two fine British battleships, *Triumph* and *Majestic*, have been sunk before your own eyes by submarine boats, all protective means against them being found utterly insufficient.

Since those severe losses to the British Navy your men-of-war had to take refuge and have abandoned you to your fate.

Your ships cannot possibly be of any help to you in future since a great number of submarines are prepared to suppress them.

Your forces have to rely on sea transport for reinforcement and supply of food, water, and every kind of war materials.

Already the submarines did sink several steamers carrying supplies for your destination.

Soon all supplies will be entirely cut off from your landed forces.

You are exposed to certain perdition by starvation and thirst.

Even desperate attacks will not avert that fate from you.

You could only escape useless sacrifice of life by surrendering. We are assured that you have not taken arms against us by hatred.

Greedy England made you fight under a contract.

You may confide in us for excellent treatment.

Our Country disposes of ample provisions; there is enough for you to feed you well and make you feel quite at your comfort.

Don't further hesitate! Come and surrender.

On all other fronts of this war, your own people and your allies' situation is as hopeless as on this Peninsula.

All news spread among you concerning the German and Austrian armies are mere lies.

There stands neither one Englishman, nor one Frenchman, nor one Russian on German soil.

In the contrary the German troops are keeping a strong hold on the whole of Belgium and on conspicuous parts of France, since many a month.

A considerable part of Russian Poland is also in the hands of the Germans who advance there every day.

Early in May strong German and Austrian forces have broken through the Russian centre in Galicia. Przemysl has fallen back into their hands lately. They are not in the least way handicapped by Italy's joining your coalition, but are successfully engaged in driving the Russians out of Galicia.

These Russian troops whose co-operation one made you look forward to, are surrendering by hundreds and thousands. Do as they do! Your honour is safe! ! Further fighting is mere stupid bloodshed!!!

In spite of the fact that there was no large attack for nearly a month, the field ambulances were crowded with a constant stream of wounded, both from the rest camps and from the trenches.

The distance from the firing line to the beaches was less than five miles, and consequently its whole extent was open to shell-fire both from the Achi Baba direction and the Asiatic coast. The rest camps were under direct observation, and even a small collection of men was certain to provoke shell-fire.

Few of us will ever forget those endless journeys up to the trenches, the long stretch across the open, the comparative safety of Backhouse Post where the wide mule track commenced, and the final narrow communication trench leading to the firing line—always to the same accompaniment, the tramp of feet, the ceaseless croaking of frogs in the river bed, the *zip* of bullets hitting the sandbags, and the joking, laughing, and not in-frequent swearing of the men. How cheerful and incomprehensible they all were—enduring incredible hardships with a careless jest and then grousing over some triviality—'Ere! 'oo's bent my bleedin' bayonet? If I want it bent, can't I do it myself in a bloomin' Turk?' was the remark made by a fellow who thought nothing of 'going over the top' but could not bear to think of anyone using *his* bayonet to dig a dugout or open a bully beef tin!

Such were the players and the scene, and if you add a scorching sun, flies, and smells, a clear idea of the play is obtained, at any rate in its more peaceful aspect.

Past an open space, dotted with the graves of men killed in the earlier fighting, was the Lancashire Dressing Station, and further on again 'Brown House'—the meeting of many ways and the site of one of our bearer posts, a large ammunition and supply dump, and the headquarters of a reserve battalion.

The traveller reached the front line tired, irritable, and dripping with perspiration, sat down limply on the fire-step, vainly attempted to drive the flies away from his vicinity, and in the intervals of bemoaning his fate unconsciously listened to the cheerful chatter of the men, until finally he him-self became infected with their cheery good humour. 'Sweaty 'ot, ain't it?' said Bill to Alf, expectorating over the parapet with deadly accuracy. 'What about a pint o' beer?' 'Not 'arf, not for me, thanky; couldn't touch it, supposin' it was 'anded to me and you payin'.' Swear, I should think they did, but no offence was meant and none taken. Most of their terms might have shocked a mothers' meeting, but when interpreted, they were merely terms of endearment, common to a seafaring race.

In the fire trenches there was much of interest—sniping through loopholes or with a periscope rifle, and firing hand-grenades from prehistoric-looking catapults, said to have come from Carnage's; but however the scene might vary, always the same intense heat, overpowering smells, and ubiquitous flies. How those flies pervaded everything! Food became black with them immediately it was uncovered. They swarmed around the unburied dead and infested the habitations of the living. They spoilt the temper of the healthy and added greatly to the sufferings of the wounded and sick. No wonder men ate little. Unopened bully beef tins were stuffed in the parapet for want of a better use—meat for the asking, and yet few had any desire to touch it. Tins of jam in plenty, but none cared to sample them, except perhaps the Turks, to whom we slung them over in our catapults. Tickler's artillery, named after a firm of jam makers, soon became famous. It consisted of 'plum and apple' tins, emptied of their legitimate contents and filled with high explosive, odd lumps of metal, and a detonator. These had a destructive effect out of all proportion to their harmless appearance.

FRONT LINE TRENCH AT HELLES

WITH THE M.E.F. AT
HELLES

June 4th at last arrived. It was the day of the *great* push, from which so much was expected and which proved such a bitter disappointment. The bombardment commenced at 8.30 a.m., and with only two short intervals continued until noon, when a general advance was made all along the line. On the right, the French stormed the Haricot Redoubt, whilst the Royal Naval and 42nd Divisions gained their objectives, but on the left both the 29th Division and Cox's Indian Brigade were unable to go forward any appreciable distance. Unfortunately the French, in face of repeated strong counter-attacks, had to evacuate their new positions, and the Collingwood Battalion, which was on their immediate left, was hence caught by enfilade fire and almost annihilated. The first wounded were cheery and full of the great success they had gained, but as time went on, and fresh batches arrived, the spirit of optimism gave place to one of shattered hopes, and they had no knowledge of victory to help them bear the pain of their wounds, the intolerable flies and the sickly smell of blood in those dirty, stuffy aid posts, most of which were no more than an unoccupied portion of trench. The dressing-stations and the trenches leading to them were full of wounded, and it was more than twenty-four hours before they were all evacuated to the beach.

In spite of the optimistic reports on the action in the *Peninsular Press*, it was evident that all hope of a speedy termination to the campaign was ended, at any rate, for the time being, and that siege warfare must now be inevitable.

On the following day, D Company of the Nelson Battalion advanced over the open and dug the celebrated Nelson Avenue. It was a fine piece of work, but cost four officers and seventy-six men. The Turks eventually gained a footing in the northern end of this trench, but were quickly driven out by an heroic little party of nine men, armed only with picks and shovels.

On June 18th the Hawke Battalion attempted, but without success, to capture an isolated piece of trench lying in front of their line. The Portsmouth Marines finally stormed the position, but finding it full of dead and uninhabitable, contented themselves with merely filling it in.

The two main features of the remaining days of June, from a military standpoint, were the taking of the Haricot Redoubt by the French on the right flank, and the capture of a system of trenches one thousand yards deep by the 29th Division on the left flank. These two successes were of considerable importance as, by bringing up the flanks, the whole line was straightened.

From a medical standpoint, this month was remarkable for a large and sudden increase in sickness. Gone were the healthy days of April and May, and with the increasing heat numerous epidemics arose. Chief amongst these were typhoid, paratyphoid, dysentery, enteritis, jaundice, malaria, and that obscure condition known in the army as P.U.O. (pyrexia of uncertain origin). The 'Gallipoli Gallop' was a term largely used by the men and covered any complaint of which the words are suggestive or symptomatic. The amount of sickness was so great that the division, in spite of numerous reinforcements which continually arrived, would soon have become non-existent if every sick man had been evacuated to hospital. Hence all who could carry on at all were kept with their battalions, and treated by the battalion medical officers. The men, with a very fine *esprit de corps*, appreciated the adverse conditions under which we laboured and made light of their complaints.

About this time the 52nd Lowland Division landed, and were placed in reserve to the Royal Naval Division. Their surprise at the small size and comparatively insignificant appearance of Achi Baba was intensely amusing. They had been gravely assured in England that it was a mighty mountain, and found instead a gently undulating slope which from the rest camps scarcely appeared to be a hill at all. 'What kin' o' a place is yon? That wee bit hill is no Achi!' exclaimed a stalwart Scotch sergeant, and intimated his intention of sending a small fatigue party from his platoon to capture it that very night. Their ideas were somewhat modified by having a large number of casualties before reaching even the reserve trenches, and very soon they fully appreciated the many modestly concealed properties of Achi Baba.

On the morning of July 12th, after a heavy bombardment of many hours, the Scottish battalions made a very gallant attack. In places it met with great success, but owing to the loss of certain small parts of our gains and especially of those isolated posts which threatened the safety of the remainder of the line, the Royal Naval Division was ordered to counter-attack. After a short bombardment at 5 p.m., the order 'Stand by to advance' passed down the line, and a few minutes later the Naval Division swept over the top, and in the face of a murderous machine-gun barrage, took their objectives at the point of the bayonet. Though supremely successful, our losses were exceedingly heavy and included two battalion commanders, Lieutenant-Colonel Evelegh, and Lieutenant-Colonel Luard, who were both killed.

Windmills of   Hill 200   Achi Baba   Taylor's Post
Krithia

Dug-outs of the 2nd (R.N.) Field Ambulance
in foreground

Outstanding amongst the many brave deeds of that action was the manner in which Lieutenant Murdoch Browne, Royal Marines (since killed at Beaucourt), gained his D.S.C. for holding a portion of trench for two days and two nights without food or water, until he and four men, all wounded, were the only remaining survivors of his platoon.

On the following day, owing to some mistake, a certain regiment retired, leaving their first and second lines entirely unoccupied. Major Sketchley of the Royal Marines, ably assisted by Lance-Corporal Way, appreciated the very critical state of affairs, and rallying the men, led them forward in a very able and gallant manner to reoccupy their trenches. He undoubtedly saved what was quickly becoming a very serious situation, and for his resource and coolness was awarded the D.S.O., whilst Lance-Corporal Way gained the C.G.M.

Simultaneously with our attack, the French advanced on the right and took over five hundred prisoners. Many of them passed through my aid post, and were all in a state of the most abject fear, falling on their knees before us with discordant shrieks for mercy. Those who were wounded bore their pain manfully and were very grateful for any attention or kindness, making it very obvious that they had been wilfully misinformed as to the reception they might expect from the Allies when captured. One wounded prisoner, a fine fellow over six feet in height, came to me at Brown House to be dressed. There he sat, with a large jagged bayonet wound in the neck, making no complaint, although pale from loss of blood and looking very wasted and ill; he just smiled to himself and took stock of all around him. He informed our interpreter later—and I think it shows how short of men they were—that he was one of a draft that had arrived the previous night after a fifteen-days' march from Adrianople. He mentioned also that the draft consisted of inferior troops, although his appearance would seem to have given the lie to this statement.

Although a successful action, our casualties were enormous. In addition to a very large number of killed and missing, nearly two thousand wounded passed through the aid posts of the R.N.D. alone. Whole companies had been cut off, surrounded and killed or captured, but though the loss of so many friends made one's outlook somewhat jaundiced, still I shall always think that this was the time when the Turk was at his lowest ebb. For some weeks he had shown very little of the initiative that distinguished his earlier tactics, and the prisoners in the last battle were undoubtedly demoralised. A Turkish order captured about this time confirms the impression:

. . . Henceforth commanders who surrender trenches, from whatever side the attack may come, before the last man is killed, will be punished in the same way as if they had run away. . . . .
. . . Henceforth I shall hold responsible all officers who do not shoot with their revolvers all the privates who try to escape from the trenches on any pretext.

Unfortunately our artillery was never adequate to cope with the maze of hostile trenches and redoubts—a system so intricate that it was almost impossible to chart it accurately, and this seemed largely to account for our casualties. Had it been possible to treat these trenches to a bombardment, such as usually precedes an advance in France—one of days or weeks rather than hours—Achi Baba would have been taken when and how we liked. By the end of July the British casualties approached 50,000—8000 killed, 30,000 wounded, and 11,000 missing, and the French casualties were equally heavy.

On August 6th we opened a general bombardment and made numerous small local attacks in order to distract attention from the landing which was in progress at Suvla, but after that date there was very little actual fighting at Helles, except a small local operation very successfully carried out in November by the Scots. About this time it was decided to reform the division and amalgamate various battalions, reducing our strength to two brigades which were ordered to hold the left centre sector in front of Krithia.

Bombing, trench mortar activity, mining and counter-mining, were now the order of the day. The 29th Division were the originators of mining in Gallipoli, but it soon became general except in the sector occupied by the French, who adopted the very reasonable attitude that, if you leave the Turk alone, he will leave you alone. Personally I could never appreciate what material advantage we gained from our labours, nor did I ever meet any one who was particularly enthusiastic over the work, with the very notable exception of the O.C. Mines, 8th Corps—one of the most ingenious of men, who constantly sprang surprises both on us and the unfortunate Turks. On one occasion, I accompanied him in his tour of inspection of a gallery at the head of Gully Ravine in the sector then occupied by the 42nd Division.

After climbing down innumerable rough steps, bumping my head continually, and crawling on all fours along dirty subterranean passages, we eventually came to a listening post, where I was told to put my ear to an instrument looking like a battered gramophone horn, and rejoicing in the name of a tympanum. It was indeed a most weird and uncanny sensation to hear the Turks tapping away at one of their near-by shafts and wondering when they would blow us up. I was assured that we usually 'blew' first, but unfortunately this occasion proved to be an exception to the rule, as without the least warning there was a terrific explosion, and I found myself hurled to the ground, where, in the intervals of collecting my scattered senses and belongings, I vaguely wondered what in the world could have happened.

My guide reassured me that nobody was hurt, and aching in every limb, I climbed up to the top of the shaft, and looking over the para-pet, saw the results of the explosion, a crater of over fifteen feet in di-ameter. It was undoubtedly an interesting experience, but hardly one to encourage curiosity in the future. Only a few days later this very gallery was blown in and three men entombed. They succeeded after sixty-five hours in digging themselves out with only one pick and no shovel, food, water, or light—an achievement of no mean order, and one which was put on record in the Corps Orders of the day.

By the end of October 1915, the Gallipoli Campaign had become purely a secondary operation, the object of which was merely to keep a large number of Turkish troops in Gallipoli, who otherwise would have been sent to reinforce our enemies in Mesopotamia or the Cau-casus. Our reverse in Gallipoli and the disastrous Russian retreat in Poland, could hardly be expected to impress neutral states, and as a consequence, Bulgaria declared war on Serbia, and Greece, in spite of her treaty obligations, continued to maintain an attitude of hostile neutrality.

With the Bulgarian intervention and the invasion of Serbia came the opening of communications between Turkey and Central Europe, with the inevitable result that the Turks could now get an adequate supply of ammunition, and consequently our positions were daily exposed to very heavy shelling. To add to our troubles the weather, which up till now had been continuously fine, began to break. On November 21st a torrential downpour commenced, and soon all the dugouts were flooded and the gullies became raging torrents. This was followed by a blizzard, during which all the piers were damaged, and some even completely blown away.

CHAPTER 6

Imbros, Suvla, and the Attack on Koja Chemen Tepe

How went the day? We died and never knew.
But, well or ill, England we died for you!

After the action of July 13th, the 2nd (R.N.) Field Ambulance, to which I was then attached, was sent to the Island of Imbros for a much needed rest. Following on so many months in Gallipoli, it was a very pleasant change to live under conditions of comparative peace, though the dust and heat were quite as bad here as they had been in the peninsula. Most of the rest camps were situated near Kephalos Bay, the broad, flat, sandy shore of which was dotted with innumerable camps and hospitals full of new arrivals, men on leave or sick, who had been evacuated from Gallipoli. There was here, as at Cape Helles and Lemnos, the usual polyglot gathering of Britishers, Indians, Greeks, and Egyptians. The Egyptian Labour Corps had been recruited mainly in Alexandria, and was designed for work at the base. They worked well, but always to the accompaniment of some dreary, droning chant. As their medical officer had fallen ill, I had for some days the questionable pleasure of attending to their infirmities, a difficult undertaking, as my predecessor, an Egyptian, relied on necromancy and charms, rather than the knife and drugs, and also a thankless one, as on recovering they invariably thanked God and not their doctor.

Our main relaxation at Imbros was to ride across the hills and explore the inland villages. Six miles away was the little town of Panaghia, reached by a track which wound up the undulating hillside, affording a gorgeous view of the clear, babbling brook in the valley beneath, dotted with olive groves, vineyards, and an occasional small

TYPES OF INDIAN EXPEDITIONARY FORCE

red-roofed farmhouse. It was indeed a place where every prospect pleases and only man (referring to the dirty, unkempt natives) is vile.

Panaghia is a pretty village consisting of white cottages nestling amongst fig and olive trees which give a pleasing shade to its narrow streets, the deep shadow contrasting strongly with the sunlight that here and there pours through a gap, lighting up the brilliant dresses of the women. The greater part of the village stands on the side of a hill, at the top of which is a ruined mosque which was used until a few years ago, but is now rapidly falling into disrepair. At the foot of the hill is the Orthodox Greek Church, a long oblong building fronted by an imposing colonnade and decorated inside with numerous crude religious paintings. Two miles distant from Panaghia, and connected with it by a good metal road, is Castro, the main port of the island. It closely resembles its namesake at Lemnos, and like it, is situated on the shores of a bay flanked by a hill with mediaeval remains on the summit. The only other village in the island of any importance is Cheinoudi. It is about ten miles from Panaghia, and can be reached by a road which the Turks built for military purposes before the last Balkan War. This road, though good in places, is rarely used by the peasants, who much prefer the rough tracks across the hills to which their hardy mountain ponies are so well accustomed.

Cheinoudi is a pretty little village, and in its numerous *cafés* a passable lunch of the chicken and omelet variety is readily obtained. We found the inhabitants exceedingly obliging, but unfortunately they failed to understand the ancient Greek we had so laboriously learnt in our schooldays, and their stock of English only consisted of 'Turkey no good' and 'Turkey feeneesh.' Apparently they were ardent Venezelists—at least every house was decorated with large, badly drawn pictures of this statesman, side by side with wonderful representations of the Balkan War, portraying King Constantine mounted on a fiery Arab steed, or Greeks and Turks in the throes of battle, with gigantic red, black, and yellow shell-bursts all around. The narrow streets were thronged, not only with people, but also with fowls, pigs, and dogs. The younger men, as in most eastern countries, had little or nothing to do, and spent their time smoking and drinking in the *cafés*, whilst the women and old men were busily occupied spinning, washing clothes, or working in the fields. The only other place of interest in the island was the Turkish prisoners' camp, where, through the kindness of the commandant, I was allowed to make a few sketches.

During our three weeks at Imbros, various rumours of a fresh

EGYPTIAN LABOUR CORPS

landing were, of course, current, but so jealously guarded was the plan of operations that even those of us who were to take part in it did not know the exact whereabouts until the morning of the attack. Numerous ruses were adopted to deceive the Turks as to our intentions— troops were concentrated at Mitylene and the island ostentatiously inspected by Admiral de Robeck, maps of Asia Minor were printed in Cairo and allowed to fall into the hands of the enemy, and our patrolling vessels daily carried out range-finding practices between Anzac and Kum Kale. The Turks undoubtedly did not expect a landing at Suvla, and were taken completely by surprise.

Though the Anson Battalion, attached temporarily to a pack mule corps for water-carrying duties, and the 2nd (R.N.) Field Ambulance were the only units of the Royal Naval Division to take part in the venture, it may be of interest to the reader to describe this much criticised operation.

It must be clearly understood that the Suvla Bay landing was purely a diversion, the main object of Sir Ian Hamilton's plan being that the troops at Anzac, strongly reinforced, should simultaneously advance, capture Sari Bahr Mountain, cross the Peninsula, which is very narrow at that point, and seize Maidos. By so doing the Helles portion of the Turkish army would be entirely cut off. The Suvla landing was never meant to be the main feature of the operation, but was intended as a diversion to enable the Anzacs to gain their objectives. This is a fact which is not generally understood by the public, but is fully corroborated in Sir Ian Hamilton's dispatch of January 6th, 1916. In addition, there was a second diversion at Helles to prevent the Turkish army there sending reinforcements to Anzac, and a third diversion to the North of Gaba Tepe consisting of an attack on the Lone Pine trenches.

In the accompanying map, (page 79), it will be seen that Nebrunezi Point, the southern boundary of Suvla Bay, is only five miles from Anzac. The northern boundary, Suvla Point, is close to Karakol Dagh and Kiretch Tepe Sirt, a range of mountains running along the coast in a north-easterly direction and then curving inland as the Anafarta Hills, whose highest points are Kavak Tepe and Tekke Tepe. These hills are divided from the Sari Bahr range by a valley on the north of which is Anafarta Sagir (or Little Anafarta), and on the south Anafarta Biyuk (or Big Anafarta). This valley leads directly to the Narrows. From the plain, lying between the Anafarta Mountains and the coast, rise three hills which were of great importance in the campaign—Chocolate

A Rough Track across the Hills

Turkish Prisoners at Imbros

Hill, Green or Burnt Hill, and Scimitar Hill. Between these three hills and Suvla Bay lies the Salt Lake, with Lala Baba on its western shore.

On the evening of August 6th, 1915, our party and two battalions of the 11th Division embarked in the 'blister' ships, *Theseus* and *Endymion*, whilst the remainder of the 11th Division were taken across in transports. Just after dark we dropped anchor about a mile to the south-west of Lala Baba. The 32nd and 33rd Brigades landed to the south of Nebrunezi Point at 'B' and 'C' Beaches, and met with little opposition. The 34th Brigade landed at 'A' Beach, which lies midway between Suvla Point and the Salt Lake, and met with considerable resistance from the Turks, who were entrenched round Lala Baba and Hill 10. Through the pitch black night the Division advanced across an unknown country which afforded no cover whatsoever. They stormed Ghazi Baba, Hill 10, Lala Baba, Chocolate Hill, and the greater portion of the Karakol Dagh.

Then something seemed to go wrong. Whether the water supply ran out, or owing to lack of orders, I do not know, but one thing is certain, not only was no further advance made on August 7th, but certain vital positions on the Karakol Dagh were lost. Had we been able to advance further along these northern heights or to capture Ishmael Oglu Tepe, a protective flank for the Anzac attack on Koja Chemen Tepe would have been provided, and all might have been well. So difficult and confusing was the country that, just as in the primary landings at Anzac and Helles, many small parties of men advanced too far and got cut off. By August 9th our position was still unchanged, though in the interval the 10th Division had landed to reinforce the 11th, but two divisions were merely a drop in the ocean in a country where a few well-sited machine-guns could hold up a battalion. In brief, the Suvla landing had failed in its object.

At the same time as our landing at Suvla, the troops at Anzac, strongly reinforced, had commenced the major part of the operation. Early on August 7th they stormed Rhododendron Spur and were within striking distance of Chunuk Bair. Table Top and Bauchop's Hill were then captured, and assaulting columns advanced up the gullies of Sazli Beit Dere and Chailak Dere. The left of the line seized Damaje-lik Bair and attempted to get in touch with the Suvla forces. Everything seemed to go well at Anzac on that memorable August 7th. On August 8th the right column even reached the summit of Chunuk Bair, from where they could see Maidos and the Narrows—just one fleeting glimpse of the promised land—and then on August 10th the

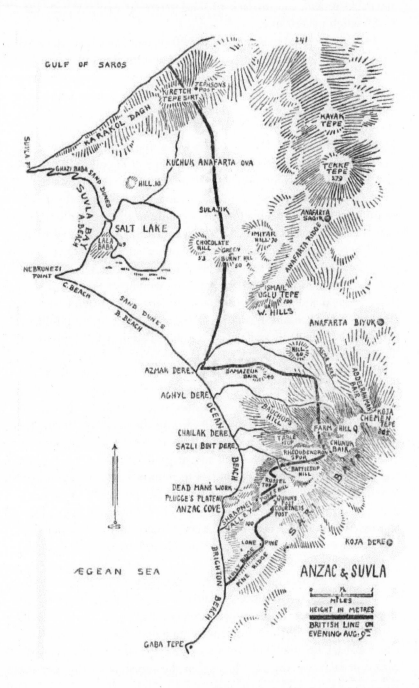

GULF OF SAROS

241

KIRETCH TEPE SIRT
TEPHSON'S POST

MARAKOL DAGH

KAVAK TEPE

KUCHUK ANAFARTA OVA

SUVLA PT.

GHAZI BABA SAND DUNES

TEKKE TEPE 279

HILL 10

SULAJIK

ANAFARTA SAGIR

SUVLA BAY
A BEACH

SALT LAKE

CHOCOLATE HILL 53

GREEN

IMITAR HILL 70

ANAFARTA RIDGE

LALA BABA

BURNT HILL 50

NEBRUNEZI POINT

C. BEACH

SAND DUNES

ISMAIL OGLU TEPE 100
W. HILLS

B. BEACH

ANAFARTA BIYUK

HILL 60

ASMA DERE

AZMAK DERE

DAMAJEUK BAIR 40

ADDERNHAM BAIR

AGHYL DERE

OCEAN

SAUCHOPS HILL

FARM HILL Q

KOJA CHEMEN TEPE 805

CHAILAK DERE

TABLE TOP

CHUNUK BAIR

SAZLI BEIT DERE

BEACH

RHODODENDRON SPUR

BATTLESHIP HILL

DEAD MAN'S WORK
PLUGGE'S PLATEAU
ANZAC COVE

RUSSEL TOP

SHRAPNEL VALLEY 100

STEELE'S POST
QUINN'S POST
COURTNEY'S POST

LONE PINE

KOJA DERE

HOLLY RIDGE
PINE RIDGE

BRIGHTON BEACH

ÆGEAN SEA

ANZAC & SUVLA

0   ½   1
MILES
HEIGHT IN METRES
BRITISH LINE ON
EVENING AUG. 9th

GABA TEPE

inevitable retreat, due to lack of reinforcements and the help from Suvla which never came.

The diversion at Helles had meanwhile been in progress and gained little success. On August 6th, the 29th and 42nd Divisions failed to capture their objectives, and on August 7th and 8th our troops were likewise unsuccessful. The remaining diversion north of Gaba Tepe was very successful, and the Lone Pine trenches were captured with great dash.

To return again to Suvla, all was not going well. On August 8th a general inaction seemed to set in, and Sir Ian Hamilton, fully recognising Turkish reinforcements were pouring in, and that there was immediate necessity for an advance, came over from Imbros with Lieutenant-Colonel Aspinal[1] on the evening of that day, only to find one brigade out of the two divisions sufficiently concentrated to advance, and that orders for a general attack could not be given owing to 'scattering of the troops.' This one brigade (the 32nd) received orders to attack immediately, and the remainder of the forces were to advance so soon as practicable towards the high ground between Ishmael Oglu Tepe, and Kavak Tepe. Preceded by an hour's bombardment, both from land and sea, at 5 a.m. on August 9th, our troops finally commenced to advance.

On the right flank a certain amount of success was met with, but, owing to bush fires and the broken nature of the ground, no material advantage was gained, and the casualties were very severe. In fact the attack only served to prove the fatal error of the inactivity during the previous day. Then there had been little artillery resistance, whereas now the Turks, having taken full advantage of our hours of inaction, had brought up many new batteries to reinforce their positions. On the following day the newly arrived 53rd Division made a further attempt to capture the Anafarta Hills, but failed to achieve their object, and by August 11th it was obvious to all that we had shot our bolt, and hence orders were issued to entrench and consolidate the positions already gained.

The outlook was now exceedingly depressing. The early stages of the landing appeared so successful and our hopes ran high, but now the sands of time were fast running out and we had failed. In the scheme of operations, the 11th Division were intended to capture Lala Baba, Ghazi Baba, Chocolate Hill, Ishmael Oglu Tepe, and Kiretch Tepe Sirt before daylight of August 7th, and on the morning of that day the

---

1. Later Chief Staff Officer of the R.N.D.

10th Division were to land, capture Anafarta Biyuk, and link up with the Anzacs on Sari Bahr. How little were these hopes fulfilled!

Further attempts were made to break through, notably on the 15th, 21st, and 27th August, but the enemy had so strengthened his position in the interval, that our efforts were doomed to failure.

The 2nd (R.N.) Field Ambulance had in the meantime been busily engaged evacuating wounded from Chocolate Hill and Burnt Hill to the beach, but towards the end of August orders were received to move to Karakol Dagh. The night was spent wearily plodding along the shore of the Salt Lake, and our arrival did not receive the gratifying amount of attention we would have liked. No one seemed to know or care anything about us, and so, gloomily manhandling our gear, we toiled up the hill, quite unconscious of the fact that it was entirely under enemy observation. This truth was forcibly brought home to us by the sudden appearance of an irate fellow from a neighbouring dugout, who in no measured terms gave us to understand that he did not care if *we* were shelled to Hell, but that, as he lived there, he did not want shells dropping round *his* home.

Having sampled various sites and been driven from each in turn, we ultimately settled down towards evening in a shallow dip on the southern slope of Karakol Dagh, and there formed a dressing-station about a mile from Jephson's Post. The line of evacuation from here to the beach was very steep and rugged and covered with stiff thorny scrub. For the greater part of the way the path ran along the crest of the hill. On the northern side was the precipitous cliff falling abruptly down to the Gulf of Saros, whilst to the south there was a more gradual descent towards the Salt Lake. The summit commanded a magnificent view of the underlying plain, a splendid sight when the sun was setting behind Samothrace, the prominent parts of Anzac and Sari Bahr glittering in its golden rays.

I used to sit outside the door of my aid post and have a quiet yarn with an N.C.O. of my acquaintance—a curious and interesting fellow who spoke in an absent-minded manner, reminiscent of the night watchman in Jacobs's tales. *A propos* of nothing in particular he would say, 'I used to go to Sunday School until I was twenty-six. Aye, we used to have play-actin' and dancin' and all kinds. Every year we gave a play, sometimes Joseph and his Brethren, other times Queen Esther. Expense! There weren't no expense about Joseph; he only 'ad to 'ave a white cloak and *putties* round his legs, but Queen Esther was different; she 'ad to 'ave tights.' I have always wanted to see their interpretation of these biblical stories, and intend to take a trip to Lancashire for this purpose, if and when the war ends.

When the inevitable trench warfare set in, little of interest occurred at Suvla. We were unable to attack, and the Turks were apparently unwilling to attempt the experiment of driving us out of our entrenched positions. They, however, kept up a continuous bombardment of our rest camps, dumps, and piers, which, as at Cape Helles and Anzac, were never out of range. It will always be a matter of surprise to me that our casualties were so small in those days. A shell would drop with a loud *crum-pp*, and when the cloud of dark smoke had cleared away, men and horses could be seen running in all directions, with an occasional huddled figure lying unnaturally on the beach. Sometimes a shell caused great havoc. I well remember a high explosive shrapnel which killed or wounded upwards of seventy men, but this was distinctly rare.

At the beginning of October orders were received for the 2nd (R.N.) Field Ambulance to embark for Helles. We left Suvla Bay with few pleasant memories, and all very pleased to rejoin again the main part of our division. Just as we arrived at 'W' Beach, the news of the great push at Loos had been announced to the troops. From all sides came the sound of singing and cheering, the skirl of the bagpipes from the Scottish Rest Camp, and the crash of the guns firing a regular salvo in honour of the great event.

PRELIMINARY BOMBARDMENT AT SUVLA BAY

CHAPTER 7

The Evacuations of Gallipoli

SPECIAL DARDANELLES ARMY ORDER OF THE DAY, DARDANELLES ARMY HEADQUARTERS, 11TH JANUARY 1916.

The Army Commander has much pleasure in publishing, for the information of all ranks, the following gracious message which has been received by the Commander-in-Chief from His Majesty the King:

> It is with feelings of intense satisfaction that I have just heard of the successful evacuation of Helles. Please accept for yourself and convey to General Birdwood, General Davies, and the troops under their command my hearty congratulations on this fine performance. I am confident that these splendid units from Anzac, Suvla, and Helles will renew in fresh fields of action the hard-won and glorious traditions won in Gallipoli.
>
> George, R.I.

The landings at Anzac and Suvla were both doomed to failure, but the positions had to be held until a suitable opportunity to evacuate them should arise. On December 8th, 1915, Lieutenant-General Birdwood, G.O.C. Dardanelles Army, received orders to proceed with the evacuation without delay. At the time of the Suvla and Anzac withdrawal, the Royal Naval Division was at Helles, and so I am unable to give a full description of what actually occurred. It may, however, be of interest briefly to quote a few details from the dispatch of Vice-Admiral Sir R. E. Wemyss, dated December 22nd, 1915. The evacuation was carried out in three stages.

1. December 10th. A preliminary stage during which all per-

sonnel, animals, and vehicles not necessary for a winter campaign were removed.

2. Night of December 17th-18th—during which all personnel, guns, and animals which were not absolutely necessary for the defence of the positions, in the event of an enemy attack, at the last moment were removed. These consisted of 200 guns, 3000 animals, and 44,000 men.

3. Nights of December 18th-19th and 19th-20th—the final stage, which included the embarkation of all personnel remaining and of all guns and animals not previously withdrawn. During this period 10,000 were taken off from each beach on successive nights.

At Anzac the evacuation was complete at 4.15 a.m., and at Suvla at 5.39 a.m.

******

After the evacuation at Suvla and Anzac, an official announcement was made that we should hold on at Cape Helles.

Printing Section,
Med. Exped. Force,
G.H.Q.

SPECIAL ORDER OF THE DAY, BY LIEUTENANT-GENERAL SIR FRANCIS DAVIES, K.C.B., COMMANDING 8TH ARMY CORPS, GALLIPOLI PENINSULA, 20TH DECEMBER 1915.

The British troops have been removed from Suvla and Anzac in order that they may be more usefully employed elsewhere to defeat German ambitions in this theatre of war and to crush the Turks and Bulgars who have been induced to join our enemies. This withdrawal was carried out entirely unknown to the enemy, and thanks to the steadiness and discipline of the troops and to the excellent arrangements made by the Staffs of both Navy and Army, nothing has been left to the enemy but our empty trenches. A few guns at Anzac which could not be extricated from their positions were destroyed.

The position at Cape Helles will not be abandoned, and the commander-in-chief has entrusted to the 8th Corps the duty of maintaining the honour of the British Empire against the Turks in the Peninsula and of continuing such action as shall prevent them, as far as possible, from massing their forces to meet our main operations elsewhere.

This duty is one for which we are fully prepared, and is only the continuation of the operations which have gained the strong position we now hold. In front of this position division after division of the Turkish army has been worn down, and so many Turks have been killed that this part of the Peninsula is known amongst them as 'the Slaughter-House.'

We can only hope that the Germans will force the Turks, already heartily sick of the war, to attack us again and again, being confident that the same fate will befall all fresh troops that are brought against us as befell their predecessors.

Reinforcements of artillery and increased supplies of ammunition have already arrived, and further troops will be available shortly. In the meantime, Sir Francis Davies wishes every officer, non-commissioned officer, and man to know how confident he is that, one and all, they will put their whole hearts in the work before them, and that they will show, both to the Turks and to those at home, who are so anxiously watching our deeds, that the 8th Corps will continue to do more than pull its weight.

We must, by strenuous labour, make our positions impregnable, and while driving back every attack, we must ever seek to make steady progress forward and maintain, both in spirit and action, that offensive which, as every Soldier knows, alone leads to success in war.

H. W. Street, Brigadier-General,
General Staff, 8th Army Corps.

This statement was backed up by the fact that the 1915 Christmas card of the 8th Corps portrayed the figure of a pugnacious British bull-dog hanging on to the toe of a boot which represented the Cape Helles end of the Peninsula. December was drawing near its close when we were greeted by the following notice in Routine Orders:

8TH ARMY CORPS WILL SHORTLY BE RELIEVED BY THE 9TH A.C.

Of course everybody thought it meant the 9th Army Corps, though apparently it stood for the 9th of January—A.C. being merely a piece of necessary camouflage on the part of an astute intelligence department, or possibly the initials of the staff officer who signed the order.

In the beginning of December 1915 the French commenced to withdraw their infantry from Helles, and on December 12th the

85

R.N.D. took over the sector formerly held by the French Creoles. The evacuation of Anzac and Suvla set free a large number of Turkish guns and aeroplanes, hence there was a greatly increased activity on the Helles front. In addition, the guns on the Asiatic side appeared to be now well supplied with German ammunition, and not only enfiladed our trenches, but also shelled the beaches heavily, making the landing of stores increasingly difficult. The shelling during our last? few weeks on the peninsula was the most severe we had experienced since the early days of the landing.

It was not until the beginning of January that it was generally known we were to withdraw from our positions. From then onwards there were periods of absolute silence each night. For four hours or more at a time not a gun or rifle was fired. The Turk undoubtedly knew that we were preparing for departure, but was quite unaware of the actual date. During many of our 'silent hours' he sent patrols out to see if we were still holding the trenches, and always got a warm reception. His aerial vigilance increased, and the bombardment of our positions became daily more frequent and intense. We on our side kept up a great show of activity, and on December 29th the 52nd Division even captured a Turkish trench.

By January 4th, 1916, practically all the French troops and over ten thousand British had been quietly and expeditiously evacuated. On the nights of January 5th, 6th, and 7th still more troops left the Peninsula, and on January 9th the withdrawal was complete.

The battalion to which I was attached received orders to occupy trenches near Sedd-el-Bahr, and act as a rearguard on the memorable night of January 8th–9th. Sitting on an overturned tomb-stone in Sedd-el-Bahr churchyard, I watched our troops marching down from the trenches and being expeditiously embarked from the *River Clyde* at 'V' Beach. Gloomily I wondered if the rising storm would allow of the rearguard being taken off, but at 3.10 a.m. orders were received for us to embark, and going through the holes in the side of the *River Clyde* just as the troops had done in the historic landing, we boarded H.M.S. *Grasshopper* and pushed off. Scarcely had we started when there was a tremendous explosion from 'W' Beach—the firing of a dump of over ten tons of ammunition we were forced to leave behind. Up went lights all along the Turkish line, and soon they commenced to bombard the now empty beaches with a fury which was as ungovernable as it was harmless.

The Gallipoli campaign was now over. Though a failure, it will pass down to posterity as an exhibition of the most superb heroism and bravery on the part of all ranks. In the historic landing the Royal Naval Division played a prominent part, and, from that day, until the evacuation, were conspicuous by their bravery.

In the campaign the British army had 117,549 casualties, 28,202 of whom were killed or died of wounds, and in addition over 100,000 sick were admitted to hospital.

CHAPTER 8

Memories of Gallipoli

Where loyalty lies low in death,
And valour fills a timeless grave.
                    Scott.

The Evacuation, though such a triumph of organisation and so brilliantly successful, was a sad blow to all.

The campaign had been opened with a breezy confidence that Constantinople would soon fall, and only nine months later we were forced to evacuate our small foothold, leaving behind so many gallant dead; and somehow it seemed a great price to pay for what in the end proved to be worthless. General Sir Charles Munro, in a special order issued to the troops, very accurately described our feelings:

No soldier relishes undertaking a withdrawal from before the enemy. It is hard to leave behind the graves of good comrades, and to relinquish positions so hardly won and so gallantly maintained as those we have left. But all ranks in the Dardanelles army will realise that in this matter they were but carrying out the orders of His Majesty's Government, so that they might, in due course, be more usefully employed in fighting elsewhere for their King, their Country, and the Empire. There is only one consideration—what is best for the furtherance of the common cause.

I well remember a conference of officers on board the transport a few days before the landing. We were shown maps of Gallipoli with the fortifications marked on them, and were told the general scheme of the attack. One sentence stands out clearly in my memory. '*Our outposts will be on Achi Baba at dawn of the second day.*' It certainly seemed quite simple on paper, and how little we thought, as we listened, that the very ship in which we then were would return to Alexandria in a few days laden with wounded, and that we should never even get within a mile of Achi Baba!

Every one believed it was going to be a rapid advance, but we soon found it one of the hardest tasks that ever man had.

It is only in retrospect that events gain their true proportions, and although there were often hardships, endless work, great anxiety, and many a 'hopeless dawn,' yet there were also compensations, and many still have pleasant memories of old friends and places, perhaps never to be seen again.

Bathing in Morto Bay was always popular, in spite of the fact that for some inexplicable reason it gave the Turks great offence, and usually brought a shower of well-timed shrapnel over the devoted heads of the bathers, which sent them helter-skelter across the sand to take cover in the bordering scrub. Quite a number of casualties occurred in this way; but then, we were just as safe in the water of Morto Bay as in the rest camps, and so few desisted from the pleasant practice.

The Turk was essentially a 'clean fighter' in Gallipoli, and none of us bore him malice. He played the game as a true sportsman should, and it must be remembered that any regrettable incidents which are quoted in his disfavour were entirely the result of his having, perforce, many German officers holding high rank in his army.

When in rest camp, 'dining' with some other unit was a frequent practice and very popular, in spite of the fact that bully, in some camouflaged state, always graced the menu, and stewed fruit, toasted cheese, and rum were the main accessories.

Men from all parts of the world seemed to be gathered in Gallipoli, and it was always an interesting study to watch their customs and hear their outlook on life, which so frequently differed from our insular ideas.

We saw a great deal of the French, and very often bartered a tin of the inevitable 'plum and apple' for a bottle of their excellent ration wine. They were splendid fighters and always cheery, courteous, and good-natured. I well remember jumping into a trench when the Turks were shelling the old Krithia road, and finding myself in a French kitchen. My apologies for the havoc I had wrought were received with '*Ne vous dérangez pas, Monsieur,*' and the utmost good humour, and very soon I was taking cover with the cooks against the near wall of the trench.

The Corps *Expéditionnaire d'Orient*

Another saving grace about Gallipoli was a pleasing disregard for dress restrictions. It was not a fashionable place. Shorts, a shirt, stockings, and brogues were favoured by most, and there were no inquisitive A.P.Ms, to criticise our somewhat unorthodox appearance.

Our manners were perhaps a trifle slack; it was not *de rigueur* to salute all and sundry who wandered round the trenches. Generals often shared their scanty lunch with subalterns, and even the gilded staff occasionally, perforce, smoked woodbines. The climatic conditions and the fact that the whole of our narrow foothold was under shell-fire, and that there were no deep dugouts or other places of safety did away with all pomp and vanity, and every one became more natural and untrammelled by the conventions of civilisation.

There was always enough work to do, and sometimes, during an action, a great deal too much, when the collecting and treating of wounded lasted many a weary hour. In addition, there was always a host of sick during the quieter intervals, and so greatly did their numbers increase that it soon became the main object of every medical officer to attempt to prevent disease, as the conditions were so much against successful treatment. The number of cases seen *per diem* in my battalion, exclusive of wounded, averaged from 80 to 100 in rest camp, and from 30 to 50 in the trenches; on one occasion 25 *per cent*, of the total strength reported sick.

A very discouraging thought to every battalion medical officer was that, however efficient his arrangements might be, those of the Turks were notoriously bad—many of our trenches were captured Turkish trenches, their front line was in all places less than fifty yards distant from ours—in some places only five yards away—and all around us were putrefying Turkish corpses, perforce unburied.

It had to be recognised that flies always had access to infected material, and our main aim was to bury all such material as quickly and as thoroughly as possible. An epidemic of jaundice occurred at Helles towards the end of August. The number of cases rapidly increased, and by the end of September had reached alarming proportions, and necessitated many men being invalided to England. Trench fever and paratyphoid fever were also common. Though practically the whole battalion was inoculated against cholera, an outbreak of this disease was ever a very present menace. Firstly, the Turks undoubtedly experienced the disease, and in many cases streams flowed directly from the nearby Turkish trenches through our lines. Secondly, the Indian Mule Corps formed our transport, and it was always a possibility that some carrier of the disease, who had escaped detection in India, might infect the food which they brought up to the trenches.

Many people who have not been there look upon Gallipoli as a land of warmth and sunshine. To these individuals it may come as rather a surprise to learn that on November 30th, 1916, the thermometer registered fourteen degrees of frost, and that this caused twenty-eight cases of genuine frost-bite in my battalion alone.

The nervous strain of being under shell-fire day after day, week after week, and month after month might be expected to cause a large amount of mental depression and even insanity amongst the troops. This expectation was not realised in Gallipoli.

During the first six months of war, on board a battleship in the North Sea, I saw many more cases of conditions allied to melancholia than I did during my stay in the Peninsula. The mental strain of being under shell-fire appears to be much less than that of being exposed to the hidden dangers of mines and submarines, as we knew them in the early days of war. The old illusion that no good soldier ever experiences fear is, I think, entirely shattered. The modern soldier, sitting inactively in a trench or shell-hole, which is being intensely bombarded by enemy artillery, admits, not only to himself, but also to his friends, that he is frightened. In Gallipoli he knew that whether in rest camp or in the trenches any moment might be his last. The philosophic attitude with which the men faced this fact was beyond all praise.

Being only human, they were frightened and admitted it, but never did they allow this fear to interfere with the carrying out of their duties. They saw themselves as others saw them. They knew that they were not supermen merely because they wore the King's uniform, but admitted that the instinct of self-preservation was still strong within their breasts. Instead of wasting their time vainly trying to convince themselves that fearlessness is the most valuable attribute of a soldier, all frankly admitted that there was no disgrace in fear, but that the unsoldierlike thing was to let their actions be influenced by this very natural state of fear.

Not only their courage and inherent sense of duty, but also a keen sense of humour, helped to pull them through many trying times. It was only necessary to talk to them to see it. They were full of that infectious humour which compels laughter, and could even make their jests in verse. During the war I have seen many instances of this so-called poetry, but rarely a more realistic epitaph than this:

Here lies the body of a Turk unknown

Whose spirit to Kingdom come has flown.
He robbed the dead without a doubt,
But evidently lost his way about.
To regain his trench he vainly tried.
But the Royal Marines saw him and so—he died.

It was stuck over the body of a dead Turk who formed part of the parapet wall in Worcester Flat (Helles).

All who passed had their attention directed to it by the fact that the afore-mentioned Turk was—somewhat elderly.

A pleasant reminder of our Gallipoli days was received on January 1st, 1918, from our old Corps Commander, Lieutenant-General Sir Aylmer Hunter-Weston:

> To every Officer, Warrant Officer, Non-Commissioned Officer, and Man of the R.N. Division who served on the Gallipoli Peninsula:
>
> On this day of the New Year I send to all my old comrades, who served with me on the Gallipoli Peninsula, my greetings and best wishes.
>
> You did grand service to the State in that historic episode, and I esteem myself fortunate to have been associated with the Naval Division in that great enterprise.
>
> Those of us who shared the dangers and difficulties of those days together must always have a closer tie to one another than other men, and I send to each individual officer, warrant officer, non-commissioned officer, and man who was with me then, my heartiest greetings and good wishes for his welfare both in 1918 and always.

A MEMORY OF GALLIPOLI

THE SALONIKA FRONT

frontiers ――――
roads ·········
railways ――――
miles 0 5 10

CHAPTER 9

The Salonica Line

The isles of Greece, the isles of Greece,
Where burning Sappho loved and sung,
Where grew the arts of War and Peace,
Where Delos rose and Phoebus sprung.
Eternal summer gilds them yet.
But all, except their sun, is set.

Byron.

By October 1915 the Mediterranean Expeditionary Force had been divided into two distinct portions—the Dardanelles army to carry on in Gallipoli, and the Salonica army to reinforce the Serbians in their heroic attempt to stem the Austro-Bulgarian invasion. The latter force consisted of the 156th French Division from Helles under General Bailloud, the 10th Division from Suvla under General Sir Brian Mahon, and a brigade from France. This, inadequate as it may appear, was the full extent of the Salonica army, and considering how badly the greater part of it had been crippled by disease and hard fighting in Gallipoli, and remembering that the Serbian defeat was practically an accomplished fact, there is small cause for surprise that the first and principal object of the campaign was not achieved.

It was, however, imperative that something should be done and done quickly, and these were the only troops available. They landed at Salonica on October 5th, 1915, with the consent of M. Venezelos, the Greek premier, and greatly to the joy of the hard-pressed Serbians, who expected much from this Anglo-French expedition. The success which might have been attained was entirely prevented by the fact that M. Venezelos was forced by King Constantine to resign his office. With him went all hope of help and sympathy from the Greeks. Every

95

obstacle which could be devised was made by them. They cut the telephonic communications, delayed our railway transport, and conducted a general policy of obstruction and subterfuge, with the result that Uskub, which had been most gallantly defended by the Serbians, was captured by the enemy on October 9th before help could arrive, and our allies were forced back to Veles.

On October 14th, General Sarrail advanced up the Vardar Valley in the hope of relieving this town. Owing, however, to the length of his communications, the unfriendly attitude of the Greek government, and the small number of men at his disposal, he could only reach Krivolak, and on October 28th Veles, after a most heroic defence, fell into the hands of the enemy. The Serbians failing in their attempt to retake the town, commenced to retreat through Albania and the Babuna Pass. The French made every effort to get in touch with them, but being unable to capture Mount Archangel from an enemy which was in much greater force, they, in turn, were compelled to retreat, and took up a position stretching from the Vardar River to Strumnitza and from thence to Lake Doiran. The portion between Kosturino and the lake was eventually taken over by the British, but on December 8th the whole line was forced to retreat into Greek territory.

The principal object of the expedition, namely, to strengthen the Serbian army and frustrate the Austro-Bulgarian advance, having failed, all that remained to be done was to occupy a defensive line in Greek territory to prevent the enemy seizing Salonica and using it as a naval base, and to wait for some future and more propitious occasion for resuming the offensive. With these objects in view, troops were landed at Stavros on the Gulf of Orfano to form the right flank of a strongly fortified system of defences running from the Rendina Gorge to Lake Beshik, linking Lake Beshik to Lake Langaza, and from Lake Langaza past Salonica to the River Vardar.

In the meantime the evacuation of Gallipoli had been successfully accomplished, and the Dardanelles army scattered to France, the Canal, and Egypt, while the Royal Naval Division garrisoned the islands of Lemnos, Imbros, and Tenedos. In February 1916 one of our brigades, under the command of General Trotman, was ordered to embark for Stavros to be attached to the 27th Division, although, incongruous as it may seem, still remaining under the jurisdiction of the Admiral of the Eastern Mediterranean.

On a cold winter's morning we neared Stavros and dropped anchor in the Gulf of Orfano. It had been freezing over night, the sun had only risen sufficiently to touch the hill-tops, and the plain was cloaked with belts of mist and shadows—altogether a most dispiriting welcome to Greece.

Stavros plain is roughly semicircular in outline and moderately cultivated by a scanty population of ignorant peasants, chiefly composed of Greeks, with a few Turks from the two small villages of Stavros and Vrasta. Densely wooded hills enclose it to the north, south, and west, whilst the seashore forms a crescentic boundary on the east. The plain has only two outlets, one along the river through the deep Rendina Gorge to Lake Beshik, and the other along the sea-shore towards the mouth of the Struma River and Lake Tahinos. Our trench system ran along the northern bank of the Rendina River across the hills known as the 'Hump,' the 'Mound,' and 'Four Tree,' and down to Lake Beshik. Motor-boat patrols guarded Lake Beshik and Lake Langaza, whilst outposts joined the intervening space and were continued from the latter past Salonica to the River Vardar. The Greek army was encamped some fifteen miles ahead of us in the vicinity of the Struma River, and the Bulgars were in front of that again at the foot of Pilav Tepe. It seemed a most anomalous position to have a presumably neutral army between us and our enemies.

Though the hills to the north commanded those on which we were entrenched, and also the plain below, it was considered impossible for the Bulgars to get guns of sufficient calibre to reach us up to these heights, owing to their extreme steepness and the dense undergrowth which covered them. The only other route for an enemy advance lay along the shore of the Gulf of Orfano, which was under direct observation of our battleships and monitors.

Everything pointed to the fact that the enemy might, at any time, make one of his characteristic thrusts, and so we were at once ordered to improve our positions. Trenches sited for defensive purposes were dug and deepened and our communications improved by making more paths up the mountain side. In spite of innumerable zigzags, the majority of these paths were exceedingly steep, and hence pack-mule was the only form of trans-port possible. A mule can negotiate the steepest track with a characteristic *sang-froid*, often craning his neck over the brink of a precipice to gather some tempting shrub with a confidence which is scarcely shared by his rider.

From the point of view of evacuation of wounded the country was well-nigh impossible, and necessitated very numerous relays of stretcher-bearers at different points on the hill-side. The only other

GULF OF ORFANO

PLOUGHING THE FIELDS AT STAVROS

method of carrying wounded was on seats at each side of a pack saddle—a mode of conveyance generally termed a *cacolet*. Ambulance wagons could only be used for the last part of the journey across the plain.

During our stay at Stavros there was no actual offensive other than the visit of three German aeroplanes, which flew over our dumps and camps, dropping bombs as they passed, but causing no material damage, the total casualties being one Greek pig. On one occasion a German seaplane, owing to lack of petrol, was forced to come down off Thasos, and was captured by our trawlers and brought into Stavros, together with its pilot and observer. We were indebted to Major Kilner, D.S.O., R.M.L.I., who was in charge of the Stavros aerodrome, for showing us this aeroplane, and also for entertaining us with true Marine hospitality on very many occasions.

In spite of much hard work preparing for a possible attack, there was nevertheless ample time to explore the surrounding country. Rarely have I seen such a variety of flowers and birds. The latter were very similar to those at Lemnos and in Gallipoli, and the following is a list of no less than seventy-five species observed by Staff-Surgeon Stanford, D.S.O., R.N.

Blackbird Great	Northern Diver	Green Warbler
Missel Thrush	Ringed Plover	Spotted Flycatcher
Robin	Red-legged Partridge	Red-backed Shrike
Crested Lark	Sparrow	Wren
Fire-crested Wren	Pigeon	Starling
Linnet	Nightingale	Redstart
Stonechat	Wheatear	Whinchat
Swallow	Whitethroat	Chiff-chaff
Blackcap	Golden Oriole	Martin
Snipe	Woodcock	Teal
Mallard	Water-Rail	Moorhen
Goose	Dove	Hoopoe
Egret	Pied Wagtail	Grey Wagtail
Great Tit	Long-tailed Tit	Blue Tit
Coal Tit	Meadow Pipit	Gt. Spotted Woodpecker
Hawfinch	Chaffinch	Goldfinch
Kingfisher	Sandpiper	Cirl Bunting
Sedge Warbler	Reed Warbler	Red-throated Warbler
Jackdaw	Rook	Carrion Crow
Hooded Crow	Raven	Blue Jay

Magpie	Nightjar	Tawny Owl
Hudsonian Chicade	Buzzard	Sea Eagle (Osprey)
Eagle	White Hawk	Martin
Kestrel	Cormorant	Shag
Herring Gull	Gt. Black-backed Gull	Common Tern

Many a time we rode along the Via Ignatia, which St. Paul is said to have traversed in days of old, and up the Rendina Gorge, in the widest part of which is the ancient monastery of Aja Maria, standing in solitary splendour on the summit of a steep hill with a gorgeous view of the under-lying plain and surrounding mountains, the hills of Thasos in the far distance rising abruptly upwards from the clear blue sea.

A mile further up the river the gorge opens into the wide, desolate plain of Lake Beshik, dotted here and there with small primitive villages. Not infrequently a well-filled bag of snipe and duck from the reed-covered marshes of the lake graced our table. On its northern shore is the hamlet of Cuchuk Beshik, a typical Macedonian village, peopled by a race undoubtedly Turkish in appearance. Their attitude was on the surface friendly, though it was sufficiently open to doubt to justify the routine order that we were all to carry firearms and keep in large parties. The *raison d'être*, apparently, was that a brigand, one Bartholojos by name, was at large, and was credibly reputed to account for stragglers with a very professional technique in the use of his knife.

The regular patrol work of this part was carried out by the Yeomanry, who frequently rode twelve or fifteen miles ahead of our lines, with no opposition either from the enemy or the inhabitants of the villages. The actual nationality of these latter individuals seemed to be in no way important. Having lived under so many different regimes, they were entirely indifferent as to who ruled them, and were only too glad to be left brawling amongst themselves in the peaceful pursuit of their own vendettas.

Our stay on the Salonica front was fortunately only limited to March and April. During these months, and even also in May, the weather is delightful. In June and subsequently it becomes unbearably hot, and after a sweltering summer a bitterly cold winter sets in. The climatic conditions make the position of the Salonica army a far from enviable one, and it should be realised that the Allies occupy the line, not because they want it, but because it is essential the Germans should not have it to form a naval base in the Mediterranean.

About the middle of April 1916, the Naval Brigade returned to Lemnos. A few weeks earlier the Admiralty had issued an order reduc-

THE MONASTERY OF AJA MARIA

ing the division to six battalions, but owing to the exigencies of the situation this was never carried into effect, and in May our two brigades embarked for France to become a portion of the B.E.F.

A BULGARIAN PRISONER

FRANCE—JUNE 1916

63RD (R.N.) DIVISION

(MAJOR-GENERAL SIR ARCHIBALD PARIS, K.C.B., R.M.A.)

188TH BRIGADE
(Brig.-General Trotman, C.B., R.M.L.I.)

1st Royal Marines
(Lieut.-Col. Stroud, C.M.G., R.M.L.I.)

2nd Royal Marines
(Lieut.-Col. Hutchison, C.M.G., R.M.L.I.)

Anson
(Lieut.-Col. Sanders, D.S.O., R.M.L.I.)

Howe
(Commander Ramsay Fairfax, R.N.)

189TH BRIGADE
(Brig.-General Phillips, D.S.O.)

Hawke
(Lieut.-Col. Wilson, C.M.G., D.S.O., M.P., R.M.L.I.)

Drake
(Lieut.-Col. Tetley, R.M.L.I.)

Hood
(Commander Freyberg, V.C., D.S.O., R.N.V.R.)

Nelson
(Lieut.-Col. Burge, R.M.L.I.)

CHAPTER 10

Early Days in France

But favour'd France,
Thou hast had many a tale of woe to tell.
In ancient times as now.

Scott.

After an uneventful voyage to Marseilles, we entrained for the north. Rarely have I seen a fairer land than that through which we passed—miles of vineyards and green fields with pink-tinted hills in the distance and a bright blue sky overhead. The people in the Midi were not so *blasé* with British Tommies as are the northern civilians, who see them daily, and our progress was truly triumphal; every station was lined with cheering crowds, who welcomed us to France and showered gifts of food and wine upon us.

The division remained for some weeks in one of the numerous concentration areas, and during this time was brought up to strength by an army brigade being attached. This brigade consisted of the 1st Honourable Artillery Company, the 4th Bedfords, the 7th Royal Fusiliers, and the 10th Dublins. The Division also became renamed, from now onwards being known as the 63rd (R.N.) Division, whilst the brigades became the 188th (1st and 2nd Royal Marine, Anson, and Howe Battalions), the 189th (Hawke, Hood, Drake, and Nelson Battalions), and the 190th or Army Brigade.

In July 1916 we took over a portion of the line in the vicinity of Bully Grenay and Aix Noulette. Little need be said of the three months spent there, as it was one of the so-called quiet sectors. Both in and out of the line we were comfortable, and had little to complain of. In the line the main diversion was what is known as 'crater jumping.' We are indebted to Lieutenant Woolley for the following description of the consolidation of a crater by a platoon under his and Lieutenant Week's command.

It was a saucy sapper, who dug a merry mine
To blow the Boche in little bits.
And 'put the wind up' poor old Fritz,
And so preserve the line.

It was a luckless subaltern got orders from H.Q.
To take a party standing by,
And lead them forth to do or die.
On the lip of that crater new.

It was a luckless subaltern dashed out (on hands and knees)
When a German flare as bright as day
Shot up and showed him where he lay
On a broken cheval-de-frise.

It was the C.J. party which followed on behind.
And the shovel clanged on the festive pick.
And the sweat on the subaltern's brow lay thick,
And the Boche, thank God, was blind.

It was a Lewis gunner who got the notion queer.
That the show would go with more of a whoop.
If he planted an accurate 3-inch group
By the cursing subaltern's ear.

It was a weary party crawled in at break of day
And the Boches smiled when the Boches woke.
And the mortar popped and the rum jar spoke.
And the trench did melt away.

Few of us will ever forget those happy times when, out of the line, we explored the neighbouring country and made friends with the local inhabitants. Who does not recall with pleasure the charming though anaemic vender of boots in Bethune; the dainty little lady who sold us identity discs in the jeweller's shop at Bruay; the delightful Blanche who looked after our wants in the *estaminet* at Hersin, and poured forth into our astonished ears wondrous tales of the doings of her *fiancé* at Verdun; or the jovial, hospitable priest of Bully Grenay who stuck to his post in spite of the shelling.

Even those marches up to the trenches remain as pleasant memories. One can still visualise the men trudging cheerily along, carrying all the impedimenta of trench warfare and happily singing—

There's a sil—ver loin—ing,
Threw ther dawk claud shoin—ing.
Turrr—n ther dawk claud in—soide out
Till ther boys come—home.

SCENE IN A QUIET SECTOR IN FRANCE

SANITARY ROUNDS

CHAPTER 11

Duties of a Battalion Medical Officer

'Tis easier for a camel to go through the eye of a needle than to bluff our medical officer.
Thomas Atkins.

There is still a somewhat general impression that an experienced doctor is wasted in a battalion or field ambulance, and that his work could equally well be done by a second or third year medical student. It is not my intention here to dogmatise on the subject, but rather to point out what the duties of a battalion medical officer are, and to let the reader draw his own conclusions.

On joining the battalion, to my intense embarrassment, I quickly discovered that a battalion medical officer was not only supposed to have a certain knowledge of medicine and surgery, but was also suspected of being an expert sanitarian and a first-class mess caterer, in addition to showing an intelligent appreciation of the tactics and strategy of modern warfare. In order to hide my colossal ignorance of certain of these very specialised subjects I had, perforce, to adopt the attitude so commonly attributed to Highlanders of saying little, but appearing to think an 'awfu' lot' until such time as I was able covertly to assimilate a little knowledge from that all-round expert, the adjutant.

The duties of a battalion medical officer are both varied and interesting. For purposes of description they may be divided into sanitary duties, medical duties, surgical duties, lectures to officers and men, instruction of stretcher-bearers, and various unofficial duties.

SANITARY DUTIES

The battalion medical officer is, first and foremost, the sanitary adviser to his commanding officer. In other words, he is medical officer of health to a wandering community of approximately a thousand souls who live under conditions absolutely unknown in civil life. Prevention of disease, *not* treatment, is what must be aimed at.

He has to see that every officer and man is fully inoculated against enteric fever. All new drafts have to be immunised, if this has not already been done in England. Weekly inspections for scabies and lice must be held, and efficient measures taken to prevent the spread of these diseases, which are both extraordinarily common on the Western Front.

Personal cleanliness must be insisted upon, and every facility given to the men for bathing and procuring clean clothing. In rest camp and billets suitable sites for washing places must be selected, and the C.R.E. persuaded to supply the necessary timber for fitting these up. In the trenches washing, as a rule, owing to lack of water, is impossible.

As the battalion moves from place to place, the water supply has to be tested—various wells being set aside for washing and cooking purposes. It may be taken as a general rule that no water in France is fit for drinking without sterilisation. All drinking water must be chlorinated in water carts before use. Strict supervision of the issue, quality, quantity, and cooking of food is a very important matter. The quartermaster is responsible for this, and I have always found that all quartermasters whom I have met are extremely competent, and take a very genuine interest in the men. Any small suggestions I make have invariably been carried out.

Food unfit for consumption must be condemned, and company cooks, who necessarily work under very adverse conditions, must be helped in every way to overcome their difficulties. Napoleon is said to have remarked that an army marches on its stomach. Most of us are more conversant with what marches on the stomach of the army, but that is a digression and will be fully dealt with in a later chapter. What I wish to point out here is that, though this aphorism of Napoleon's, as I will shortly endeavour to prove, is only partly true, still there is not the slightest doubt about the paramount necessity for good feeding when on active service. The way the Army Service Corps supplies our huge army with food is a triumph of organisation and worthy of the very highest praise.

The disposal of refuse and excreta is always difficult, and more especially so in the trenches. Some time ago, by the experience gained from three years' active service, I issued battalion sanitary standing orders, giving exact details of the method and appliances to be adopted: (*a*) in billets and rest camps, (*b*) in the trenches, (*c*) in the march and on working parties, (*d*) during an advance. Company commanders were made responsible for these orders being rigidly enforced in their company areas or sectors of the trenches. This course was very successful.

Medical Duties

In another chapter I have briefly indicated a few of the common ailments met with on active service; here I propose merely to deal with the methods of procedure. When in billets or rest camp, there is a regular sick parade at a specified time, and this is always largely attended.

In France most of the ailments are more or less trivial, but it must be remembered that the men are living under very different conditions from those which prevail in home life. In peace time practically every household has its own little supply of medicines—in some cases a lordly Burroughs and Welcome Emergency Outfit, in others merely a box of Beecham's pills—and with these remedies they cure their simple ailments—usually 'post hoc,' sometimes, perhaps, 'propter hoc' In France they have no such placebos.

In the trenches there cannot be, owing to the exigencies of the service, a definite sick parade. It is a point of honour amongst the men not to report sick in the trenches, unless they are quite incapable of carrying on. The Tommy's code is that '*swinging the lead*' is quite permissible in order to escape a tedious route march in the back areas, but that in the face of the enemy it is a heinous offence.

In the trenches men either come along to my dugout when they are off duty or more often I give them a pill from my tablet case, as I come across them during my daily tour of the sector.

It is a curious thing how few officers or men know anything at all about the etiquette of the medical profession. I was once called late at night to the bedside of a middle-aged colonel. 'Awfully sorry to pull you along here,' he said; 'I've got a —— pain in my back. Often had it before, and always found Doan's Backache Pills cured it in no time. Would you send me some along, like a good fellow?' I prescribed a mustard plaster and four grains of calomel. On visiting my patient next morning, he informed me that my treatment was 'devilish drastic,' but 'very efficacious,' and that he had written home to his wife to send out some of his favourite backache pills, which he much preferred to my 'damned tabloids.'

As so much has been written during the past four years about wounds, that any remarks regarding their nature are open to the criticism of being merely a repetition of former conclusions, I am avoiding any mention of the varied and ghastly wounds it has been my lot to treat, and propose only to describe the general principles of surgery as practised in front line trenches.

War surgery in the trenches is mainly a matter of more or less advanced first aid and quick evacuation to an immobile unit, which in practice is the casualty clearing station. Generally speaking, no major operations, except those of the utmost urgency, should be performed in a mobile unit such as a field ambulance or regimental aid post.

For purposes of description it is as well to take a hypothetical case, and follow it from the front line to England. This man belongs to a platoon which is holding a portion of front line trench. A 'flying pig' or 'rum jar' falls on the *parados* in his vicinity, and he receives a wound of moderate severity. The stretcher-bearers of his company are quickly on the scene. They apply a first field dressing, and, as he is unable to walk, carry him on a stretcher to the regimental aid post, a dugout which is as close as possible to, and equidistant from, all four companies. The battalion medical officer's main duty is how to get this man back with the least possible pain, and, if there is not a rush of cases, to dress the wound in such a way that it need not be touched until the patient is put on the operating-table of the casualty clearing station.

All serious cases are given morphia; severe bleeding is arrested by tourniquets, and splints are applied to broken limbs. Shock is treated by the application of warmth—blankets and hot drinks, with sandbags round the legs. The patient is then carried back by stretcher to the advanced dressing station of the field ambulance. This is usually about two miles behind the line, and is the nearest possible point to the line to which a motor ambulance can be brought. He continues his journey by car to the main dressing station of the field ambulance, which is usually about five miles behind the trenches. If it be a serious case and the man comfortable, he is at once sent on to the casualty clearing station by motor ambulance; if it be a slight case and there be sufficient accommodation, he is redressed and kept in the main dressing station.

The casualty clearing station is, as a rule, seven to ten miles behind the firing line. It is equipped as a modern peace-time hospital. Here all serious operations are per-formed, and as soon as the patient is convalescent, he is despatched by hospital train to the base, from where he is sent over by hospital ship to England.

The organisation for the evacuation of wounded has reached such a pitch of efficiency, that many cases arrive in England the day after they are wounded.

To go a little more deeply into the duties of the battalion medical officer, the surgical principles which he adopts may be briefly described as mitigation of sepsis, alleviation of pain, prevention of shock, and quick evacuation.

Sepsis.—Prevention of sepsis was in peace time the very foundation of modern surgery. In trench warfare it is practically impossible. As a general rule it may be said that every wound goes septic, whatever antiseptic be used, and however soon after the infliction of the wound that antiseptic be applied. The opportunity frequently arises of thoroughly cleansing a wound a few minutes after it has been received. My experience goes to prove that, whatever antiseptic be used, the result is always, in varying degree, the same, *i.e.* the wound goes septic. I have never been able to make up my mind that one antiseptic has any great advantage over another in influencing the course which a wound will take. It appears probable that the healing of wounds depends far more on the so-called 'physiological resistance' of the patient than upon the variety of antiseptic used.

In the South African War the man who put on the first field dressing and painted the wound with iodine was rightly looked upon as the saviour of the patient. The highly cultivated soil of France teems with innumerable germs which enter into every wound, and hence all that can be expected of the first field dressing in the present war, is the prevention of any *further* gross contamination.

Shock.—The vital importance of alleviating pain, and hence diminishing shock, cannot be overestimated. In the first aid treatment of all severe wounds, the medical officer must mainly concentrate his attention on combating shock. The high nervous tension of a soldier, both before and during an attack, greatly increases the degree of shock he experiences when wounded. The belief that he is invulnerable is rudely shattered, and his mental equilibrium is proportionately upset. This, in addition to the pain of a severe wound, produces the extreme degree of shock which is not met with in somewhat similar injuries in civil life.

It is an exceedingly common impression amongst both officers and men that a compound fracture of the thigh is necessarily fatal. My experience, perhaps unfortunate, is that a very large number of such cases die of shock either at the regimental aid post, the field ambulance, or in the casualty clearing station.

On one occasion I had two officers, both wounded by the same shell, and both sustaining an uncomplicated compound fracture of the upper arm. Both were treated within ten minutes of being injured, and yet both died of shock on the following day at the field ambulance. These two cases are, however, somewhat exceptional, and I only quote them to illustrate what a large factor shock can play in modern warfare.

Most cases which are given morphia early (and by 'early' I mean within half an hour of being wounded) respond in a remarkably gratifying manner.

It is difficult for anyone who has not actually seen men wounded and who has not followed the course of the cases, to appreciate fully the degree of shock which is always associated even with trivial wounds.

Looking back on three years of fighting, I must admit that my prognosis has become very much more guarded than it was when I first joined the battalion. This change is entirely due to bitter experience.

Quick Evacuation.—I have already pointed out the importance, from the patient's standpoint, of quick evacuation to the casualty clearing station. It is also equally important from the military point of view. In the trenches the battalion aid post is at best a small dugout and can contain only a very limited number of cases. The movement of troops must not be hampered by the blocking of communication trenches for prolonged periods by stretcher cases. In addition, the sight of numerous wounded men lying exposed to shell-fire in the trenches has an undesirable mental effect on their unwounded comrades.

LECTURES TO OFFICERS AND MEN

Whenever the battalion is out of the trenches, the medical officer always gives a few simple lectures to the officers and men on elementary first aid, sanitation, personal hygiene, and the prevention of sickness.

It must be remembered that a large proportion of our new army consists of boys almost entirely unversed in the pitfalls of modern life. The medical officer does his best to interest them in general principles and avoid boring them with abstruse technical details. It is exceedingly important for him to impress them with the fact that he is not a dry-as-dust scientist, but is a man of the world and knows from personal experience what he is talking about.

Once a soldier realises the whys and the wherefores of sanitary regulations he obeys them, not so much to avoid the punishment which will undoubtedly be meted out to all offenders by the battalion commander, but rather because he appreciates the principles on which these rules are based. He realises that, while his main duty is to kill Boches, he is physically unable to continue doing so unless he also wages active warfare on his equally powerful enemy—disease. His object in the line is so strongly to entrench himself that the Boche dare not attack him with any hope of success. In the same way he must adopt strong measures regarding sanitation and personal health, which will cause certain failure to the attack of the germs of disease. Each man who maintains his health helps to increase the efficiency of the British army, and consequently to shorten the war.

Various somewhat delicate questions have to be dealt with in a broadminded way. The dire effects of excessive indulgence in the pleasures of Bacchus and Venus must be discussed openly, and from a commonsense standpoint. Men must be told plainly that, quite apart from the moral point of view, it is the duty of every soldier to ensure that he is not incapacitated by disease directly caused by his harmful habits.

Whilst on the subject of alcohol, I would like to refer briefly to that very much discussed subject—the rum ration. The abuse of alcohol leads to a train of diseases which are only too well known and need not be mentioned here. The rum ration must be regarded as a food. The quantity which is served out per man can be entirely assimilated by the body, and under the present regulations it is impossible for any man to have more than his share.

In men exposed to cold, wet, shells, and all the other discomforts of trench life, it produces a sense of comparative wellbeing, makes life just bearable, and is often just the incentive necessary for hanging on to a newly captured position until relieved.

Teetotal cranks compare the effect of alcohol—even in moderation—with that of whipping a jaded horse. The analogy is *possibly* true, but they forget that even the pluckiest horse often requires the whip to make a final supreme effort at the end of a tiring day.

The issue of rum to men worn out with the mental and physical

THE RUM RATION

strain of trench life may be a method of applying the whip, but it is a mode of castigation liked by the men, and it produces the desired result with no deleterious after effects.

Care of the feet is a matter which has constantly to be impressed on all ranks. Napoleon, as I mentioned before, is reputed to have said that the soldier marches on his stomach. This tradition has been handed down in the army for many years, and is so universally accepted by all that neither officers nor men appreciate the importance of hygiene of the feet until they are taught by bitter experience. Too much trouble cannot be taken in ensuring that every man has well-fitting boots in good repair, changes his socks twice a week, and washes his feet as regularly as his face. Every man is told that he carries a field-marshal's baton in his knapsack; from a medical and military standpoint he would be a much more efficient soldier if he discarded the legendary article to make room for an extra pair of socks. In France long marches under trying conditions are very frequent, and I have always found that the vast majority of men who fall out do so on account of lack of attention to the feet. The only method of preventing this is by frequent and careful feet inspections by platoon commanders.

Young officers must be reminded that they are responsible for the welfare of their men. It is their duty to see that every member of the platoon has warm clothing, sound, well-fitting boots, comfortable billets when in rest, and plenty of good palatable food. It is not sufficient for them merely to indent on the long-suffering quarter-master. It is up to them to scour the country for these commodities, and to make friends with *Dados*, the supply officer, and the local inhabitants —much that cannot be got through Service channels can be obtained by the expenditure of a little politeness, good-fellowship, and guile. In the same way, the platoon commander must personally inspect his men's feet at very frequent intervals. It is not sufficient to order the platoon sergeant to carry on and report later. The officer must do it himself, and must do it conscientiously. All men with abraded feet must be sent up to the medical officer for treatment.

Lectures to Stretcher-Bearers.—The regulations allow of sixteen stretcher-bearers per battalion. It is not generally known to the public that these men do not belong to the R.A.M.C., but are picked from the fighting personnel of the battalion. It is an almost invariable rule that company commanders pick their best men for this work, as it needs more than the average courage to go over the top in an attack, absolutely unarmed and defenceless, and to render first aid, often

115

within a few yards of a hand-to-hand fight. Their courage is magnificent, and their work beyond all praise.

It is the privilege of the battalion medical officer to teach these men first aid, and they are always a credit to his teaching.

OTHER DUTIES OF THE BATTALION MEDICAL OFFICER

Rest billets are usually in villages just behind the line, and as a rule contain a few inhabitants who stick to their homes, seemingly oblivious of the periodical shelling and bombing to which they are subjected. The medical attention, which they and their families require, is always supplied by the medical officers of the various battalions which go back to rest there. I have had as many as twenty patients in a day, and in one village got so much *kudos* out of assisting a Frenchwoman to bring a young Frenchman into the world, that on the following night I received an urgent summons to visit a cow which was in a similar interesting condition. Unwilling to lose the esteem of my new friends, I had recourse to the famous English policy of '*wait and see*'—with, I am glad to say, eminently satisfactory results and an increased local belief in my professional attainments.

Numerous other duties fall to the lot of the devoted medical officer. In all probability he is, *ex officio*, mess caterer to the headquarters officers' mess. This is an occupation which rarely receives the gratitude it deserves. 'Toasted cheese camouflaged as welsh rabbit three times this week,' murmurs the colonel reproachfully. 'You know, Doc, I never could stand tinned salmon,' intimates the major; whilst the adjutant stoutly asserts that the coffee tastes like ditchwater 'all owing to your d——d chlorinated water, old thing.'

The work of the housewife at home, even in these days of rationing, is as child's play to that of an unfortunate mess caterer in the trenches. By a kind of *legerdemain* he is expected to produce fresh fish, new-laid eggs, and all the other delicacies of peace time. When 'Black Monday,' the settling-up day, comes, the epicures pointedly ask one another whether 'we have had anything but rations during the past week,' and whether 'that receipted tailor's bill of the Doc's has not some connection with the exorbitant mess charges.'

Such are a few of the duties—official and otherwise—of the regimental medical officer. Some of them may appear interesting, and a few of them deadly dull, but all are in the day's work, and I look upon every day I spent on active service as well worth the hardships, the dangers, the physical fatigue, and the mental strain which are necessarily associated with warfare.

The study of mankind is undoubtedly man, and one can only see man in his natural state when untrammelled by the artificial conventions of modern society. Where can this be studied better than in a front line trench, or during an attack in which death is always hovering near, often in its most revolting forms, and consequently men are seen as they are, not as they wish to appear, and not as our supercivilisation makes them appear.

CHAPTER 12

The Ancre

And I said "There is still the River, and still the stiff, stark trees
To treasure here our story, but there are only these."
But under the white wood crosses the dead men answered low,
"The new men know not Beaucourt; we are here, we know."
Beaucourt Revisited, by A. P. Herbert of the R.N.D.

Towards the end of September 1916 we left our comfortable sector in front of Bully Grenay, and moved south to take part in the great Somme offensive. It was while holding the line prior to our advance that General Paris was dangerously wounded, and his staff officer, Major Sketchley, killed. To lose our divisional commander at this critical juncture was a great blow to all. Having so successfully commanded the division since its formation in August 1914, and having endeared himself so greatly to all ranks, his loss seemed well-nigh irreparable, and none knew better than those who served under him how much the crushing defeat we inflicted on the Germans at Beaucourt-sur-Ancre was due to his previous organisation, energy, and forethought.

The fact that another attack on Beaucourt and Beaumont Hamel was imminent, appeared evident to friend and foe alike, as it was quite impossible to make the necessary concentrations and preparations in a secret fashion. A surprise attack on a large scale is absolutely impracticable in modern warfare. Behind the trenches of both combatants are lines of stationary kite balloons, in which skilled observers watch every movement of the enemy through powerful telescopes. In addition, aeroplane scouts bring back information regarding undue activity on the railways in the back areas, and movements of troops or guns towards any particular sector of the line. It may be taken for granted that the Germans were fully aware that we were going to attack, but that knowing the enormous strength of their position, which had already resisted our repeated assaults, they were confident in their ability to repel any further efforts we might make to capture their well-nigh impregnable fortresses.

The attack had been planned for October, but the weather was so unfavourable that it had to be postponed. The heavy and constant rain converted the trenches into veritable quagmires, and the roads leading to them became almost impassable, rendering a successful advance quite impracticable at that date. This delay in following up the previous successes in the vicinity, though unavoidable, enabled the enemy to reorganise his troops, regain his morale, and increase the strength of his positions. The Naval Division waited for the weather to moderate under canvas near Englebelmer, and while there, received the signal honour of being inspected by Sir Douglas Haig.

On November 9th, the weather having somewhat improved, it was decided to delay the attack no longer, and on November 11th the preliminary bombardment commenced, and continued without intermission until dawn of November 13th, when it developed into an intense barrage.

November 12th broke cold and bleak, but moderately dry. The day had come. The Royal Naval Division marched up to its jumping-off trenches, ready for the attack of the morrow. To the uninitiated the taking up of a battle position may be considered a very uneventful undertaking compared with the subsequent attack; to us on that eventful afternoon it seemed an almost impossible task.

The enemy apparently 'spotted' us going up the communication trenches and opened a very intense and accurate fire, which lasted the greater portion of the night. We had numerous casualties, including those exceedingly popular officers, Lieutenant-Colonel Sanders of the Anson, Lieutenant-Colonel Tetley of the Drake, and Lieutenant-Colonel Burge of the Nelson—all of whom were killed. By midnight the battalions had taken up their appointed positions immediately north of the River Ancre, and at dawn we were ready to advance.

119

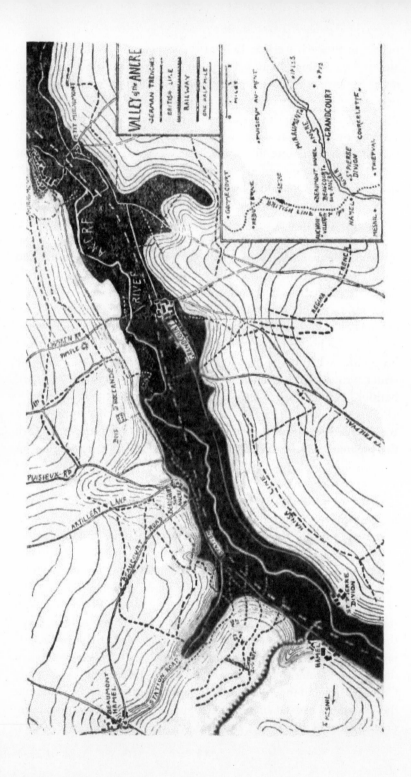

In the scheme of attack our first objective was the strong front line system of trenches, our second the Station Road, running from Beaumont Hamel to the Albert-Lille Railway, our third the trenches on the outskirts of Beaucourt, and our fourth the village itself. The 188th Brigade were on the left, the 189th on the right, and the 190th in reserve. It was a cold, gloomy, misty morning on November 13th, 1916, when at 5.45 a.m. our barrage opened in its full intensity. The men had hardly clambered out of our trenches, when the enemy barrage fell with deadly precision. In spite of heavy casualties, the Royal Naval Division, keeping close up to our barrage, which advanced one hundred yards every five minutes, swept on over three lines of German trenches, and took up a position on the far side of the Station Road and the outskirts of Beaucourt.

Numerous unrecorded incidents of that advance are still fresh in my mind. To see Sergeant Meatyard of the Marines unconcernedly following behind the attacking companies, unrolling his coil of telephone wire as he advanced, was an incident typical of the coolness displayed by all ranks. It was entirely due to his initiative that telephone communication with Brigade Headquarters was kept up during the attack. The mending of this wire, when it was once established, was a matter of no small difficulty, and all of us who reached the bank on the far side of the Station Road remember the very gallant and successful attempts made to reopen our only method of communication with the rear. Sergeant Meatyard was eventually severely wounded, and later received a very well-deserved Military Medal.

The manner in which Commander Freyberg gained his V.C. leading the Hoods to the capture of the village of Beaucourt, is too fresh in the memories of all to require repetition here.[1] How Alan Camp-

1. Brig.-General Bernard Cyril Freyberg, D.S.O.
For most conspicuous bravery and brilliant leading as a Battalion Commander.
By his splendid personal gallantry he carried the initial attack straight through the enemy's front system of trenches. Owing to mist and heavy fire of all descriptions, Lieut.-Col. Freyberg's command was much disorganised after the capture of the first objective. He personally rallied and reformed his men, including men from other units who had become intermixed. He inspired all with his own contempt of danger. At the appointed time he led his men to the successful assault of the second objective, many prisoners being captured. During this advance he was twice wounded. He again rallied and reformed all who were with him, and although unsupported in a very advanced position, he held his ground for the remainder of the day and throughout the night, under heavy artillery and machine-gun fire. When reinforced on the following morning, he organised the attack on a strongly fortified village, and showed a fine example of dash in personally (continued next page)

bell, Mrs. Patrick Campbell's gallant son, fought his trench mortar battery until all his guns were knocked out, then carried on as an infantry officer, and finally led the tanks to capture a strong point which was materially hampering our advance; how Captain Loxley, brother of that fine sailor Captain Noel Loxley of the *Formidable*, died a splendid death leading his company on to victory; how Captain Farquharson of the Marines, though wounded in the head, still pushed on with his colonel, until a sniper got him a second time, and he could walk no longer; how Surgeon Gow of the Anson dressed his wounded under a murderous fire, and after he himself was fatally wounded, spent his last hours on earth writing a report on the brave conduct of his stretcher-bearers; how that fine old Scotsman, Father Thornton, went over the top with his battalion; how seventeen men captured four hundred Germans and marched them back to our line, through both the enemy barrage and our own; and how Staff-Sergeant Carr of the 1st Field Ambulance directed the evacuation of casualties, until he was severely wounded by a sniper, are merely a few episodes of that great advance.

When I reached the Station Road above which the remains of the two Marine and Anson Battalions were digging themselves in, the only officers left in those three battalions were Lieutenant-Colonels Hutchison and Cartwright of the Royal Marines, Lieutenant-Commander Ellis and Captain Gowney of the Anson, Lieutenant van Praag and myself. All the remainder were killed or wounded, but there was no time for vain regrets. Colonel Hutchison took charge of this mixed body of men, and by his coolness, bravery, and wonderful personality, kept them cheerful and hard at work improving their position during the following two days and nights.

But to return to the actual narrative of the attack. The 189th Brigade (Hawke, Hood, Nelson and Drake Battalions) advanced along the northern bank of the river, and very gallantly captured their appointed trenches, and by noon were digging themselves in at the third objective on the outskirts of Beaucourt village. The 188th Brigade (1st and 2nd Marine, Anson, and Howe Battalions) encountered much

---

leading the assault, capturing the village and 500 prisoners. In this operation he was again wounded. Later in the afternoon, he was again wounded severely, but refused to leave the line till he had issued final instructions. The personality, valour, and utter contempt of danger on the part of this single officer enabled the lodgement in the most advanced objective of the corps to be permanently held, and on this *point d'appui* the line was eventually formed.

more severe resistance. A German strong-point, which our barrage had left untouched, entirely commanded our line of advance, and for a time completely held us up. Eventually the Anson and two Marine Battalions on the left circled round it and reached the Station Road, in front of which they dug themselves in, and connected up with the Gordon Highlanders of the 51st Division, who were advancing to our immediate north, and with the 189th Brigade to the south. The garrison of the strong-point were consequently cut off in the rear, but still their machine-gun fire hampered our movements to a large extent. Three tanks were piloted up to the redoubt by Lieutenant Alan Campbell, and at last the garrison of eight hundred surrendered.

The 13th Rifles were now ordered to reinforce the Hood and Drake Battalions, which were gallantly holding on to their gains in front of Beaucourt, and at 7 p.m. the village was stormed by this composite force under the very gallant leadership of Commander Freyberg, R.N.V.R. They dug themselves in on the far side of the village, and connected up with the 39th Division on the southern bank of the river.

In the advance everything seemed to favour the medical arrangements which had been so carefully thought out by the A.D.M.S. of the Division, Fleet-Surgeon Finch, C.M.G., R.N. We were able to take over a large German dugout along with a Boche medical officer, who rendered us great assistance until we were finally forced to send him back to the prisoners' cage. This dugout was the most sumptuous I had ever seen. It was three stories deep, and fitted with wire mattresses for over three hundred men. There were entrances from 'No Man's Land,' from the first, second, and third line trenches, and also one facing the Station Road, up to which a light railway had been laid. It consisted of innumerable small rooms, offices, kitchens, messes, and store-rooms, all of which were scattered with clothing, food, equipment and other material which had been hurriedly abandoned. One room was fitted up as an aid post, and was a model of its kind. It was lined with red canvas, lit with electric light, and replete with innumerable splints, bandages, instruments, and drugs. Opening out of this was a ward containing twelve beds where sick could be made very comfortable. In another part was what had been apparently an officers' mess, lined with a tasteful red wallpaper and adorned with pictures, a large gilt mirror, a mahogany table, and comfortable red plush chairs. Not far distant was a well-filled wine cellar and a luxurious kitchen.

In this palatial dugout we stored our casualties until the field am-

A TANK AT BEAUCOURT

GERMAN PRISONERS
FROM BEAUCOURT

BILLETS AT ENGLEBELMER

bulance stretcher-bearers arrived to evacuate them.

On the afternoon of November 15th we were relieved, and wended our weary way back to Englebelmer, our numbers sadly depleted, but every man very cheery at the thought that the Royal Naval Division had advanced further, and taken more prisoners than any other division engaged in the attack.

Simultaneously with our advance, the 39th Division, south of the River Ancre, had attacked and captured St. Pierre Divion, whilst north of us Beaumont Hamel had been successfully stormed by the 51st Highland Division.

As a result of the operation, the command of the Ancre valley on both sides of the river was secured, and in addition enormous losses were inflicted on the enemy, and his morale severely shaken by losing what he intended to be a permanent line of fortifications. The total number of prisoners taken exceeded seven thousand, including one hundred and forty-nine officers. The Royal Naval Division alone accounted for over two thousand prisoners.

After the capture of Beaucourt and the positions in its vicinity, the division was taken out of the line and sent into the back areas for a much deserved rest. The next two months were spent in reorganising and training, and on January 18th we returned to Englebelmer again fit for the line.

The 2nd Battalion Royal Marines, to which I was attached, were ordered to occupy trenches just south of the River Ancre on the outskirts of Grandcourt. Brigade Orders stated that our headquarters were to be in the village of St. Pierre Divion, but on arrival at the given map reference the village was found to be entirely non-existent, only a few scattered stones marking the site of its former glory. Our first tour in the trenches was marked by an incident which I shall always look back upon as one of the finest examples of pluck I have ever seen. Lieutenant Spinney, a corps intelligence officer, attached to us for instructional purposes, while going round our shallow front line trench, noticed that he was frequently and accurately sniped from a position some distance in front of the enemy line.

After definitely localising the sniper, he obtained permission from Lieutenant-Colonel Hutchison to attempt to capture him. Accompanied by two bombers of the Royal Marines, he crawled in broad daylight into 'No Man's Land,' and eventually found a German observation post. On getting into it he noticed a large dugout in which the garrison apparently was. Calling on them in German to surrender, he disarmed them one by one as they emerged from the dugout, and marched seven stalwart Boches back to our lines. Not content with this capture, on the following day, accompanied by Lieutenant Wren and four Marines, he attempted to repeat the procedure. Unfortunately, however, they were seen approaching, and received with a shower of stick bombs. The garrison sallied out to attack them.

The sergeant of our party, at almost point blank range, shot the leader through the head, and Lieutenant Wren neatly exploded a Mills bomb in their midst. On commencing to retreat to our lines. Lieutenant Spinney was seen lying badly wounded on the ground. Lieutenant Wren and his sergeant, both of whom were by this time wounded also, picked up their fallen comrade and made good their retreat, covered by rifle fire from the remainder of the party. Lieutenant Spinney died of wounds five days later.

As the days passed on, the shelling became more and more intense, both our back areas and trenches suffering equally severely. Many familiar landmarks were obliterated, and many of our friends killed. Amongst the casualties was that policeman, well known to the whole army, who had stood for so many months outside Mesnil Church, directing the traffic with all the *sang-froid* of a city constable.

On February 3rd, 1917, the Hawke, Hood, Drake, and Nelson Battalions attacked at midnight along the northern bank of the river, gaining all their objectives, and themselves sustaining only very few casualties. Their object apparently was to advance our line north of the Ancre, to a point level with the village of Grandcourt, which lies on the southern bank, and hence to render this stronghold untenable. In this they were successful, as on the night of February 5th a Royal Marine patrol reported that the trenches in front of the town appeared to be evacuated.

On the following morning. Lieutenant B. G. Andrews reconnoitred the position in broad daylight and confirmed this report. Lieutenant-Colonel Miller then ordered two companies of Royal Marines, under Captain Inman and Captain Cutcher, to occupy Grandcourt. This they did and dug themselves in two miles in front of our original line. The skilful manner in which this was done received great praise from all sides, including a letter of congratulation from Sir Douglas Haig.

On February 8th, the troops north and south of Grandcourt attacked to straighten the line, taking amongst other places the strongly fortified position of Baillescourt Farm.

On February 14th, the Anson, Howe, and two Royal Marine Battalions were ordered to occupy trenches near Beaucourt, in readiness for a further advance. The scheme was to seize a portion of the sunken road lying along the eastern crest of the second spur north of the Ancre, and so obtain control of the western approach to Miraumont, whilst simultaneously other troops were to capture the high ground north of Courcelette, which controls the southern approach to Miraumont.

At 5.45 a.m. on the morning of February 17th, 1917, our brigade attacked, and after severe fighting, gained all its objectives and dug itself in in the vicinity of the Pimple and the nearby sunken road leading from Baillescourt Farm.

Amongst the many incidents of this attack outstanding, was the capture of that exceedingly strong point (referred to above as the Pimple) by Lieutenant Barclay, R.N.V.R., of the machine-gun company. I visited it some hours after it was taken, and found all the evidence of a desperate fight. The dead were littered everywhere, the place was a veritable shambles and reeking with blood, and wounded were lying all round. The evacuation of these numerous casualties was carried out by Captain Anderson, D.S.O., M.C., R.A.M.C., in broad daylight under direct observation from the nearby German trenches. This officer appeared to bear a charmed life, flitting about the open under heavy fire as unconcernedly as if he were taking the air in his native city of Aberdeen. Captain Cutcher, R.M.L.I., was very conspicuous by the way he led his company, and by the skill he showed in consolidating the newly won trenches.

On February 18th, the Boche formed up to counter-attack in great force. Line upon line of grey-coated figures advanced towards us, automatically halting every few yards and firing from the hip. Major Ozanne quickly sent back the S.O.S. to our batteries, and in *three minutes* (surely almost a record) our barrage fell and annihilated the enemy. The ground we had gained was, however, of such importance that on the following day they again counter-attacked. Our barrage on this occasion opened in *four minutes* with deadly effect.

Meantime, the attack south of the River Ancre had not been so successful. The enemy, anticipating what was afoot, opened a heavy barrage some hours before the time of assault, whilst the attacking battalions were forming up in their jumping-off trenches. In spite of heavy casualties, however, they advanced with the utmost gallantry, and dug themselves in within a few hundred yards of Petit Miraumont.

On Wednesday, February 21st, the Naval Brigade was relieved, and returned to billets at Englebelmer. With reference to this attack, the following congratulatory message is quoted from Routine Orders:

The Corps Commander congratulates all ranks of the Royal Naval Division on the success of the recent operations. The preparations for the attack were most carefully worked out by all units, and success was thus assured. He thanks all concerned for the way the attack was carried out. The devotion to duty and bravery of all was splendid, and all increased the high reputation of their units. The number of prisoners captured amounts to 10 officers and 609 other ranks, which in itself is a first-class performance.

A telegram was also received from the Commander-in-Chief.

Warmest congratulations on success of your operations of 17th.

The ground gained by this attack was of such strategical importance, that the enemy was forced to evacuate Pys and Miraumont. Miraumont being in our hands rendered Serre untenable, whereas the loss of Serre made Puisieux-au-Mont and Gommecourt impossible to be held, and so, as a natural sequence, all these towns were evacuated by February 28th.

Our next few weeks were spent working hard just behind the line, in order to facilitate the British advance after this great German retreat. Though dull, this was not altogether without credit, and received the following message of commendation from the corps commander.

The Corps Commander desires to thank the Royal Naval Division for the fine soldierly spirit displayed by all ranks. Roads and railways have been constructed enabling guns and ammunition to be moved forward. The division has thereby materially contributed to the success of today's operations, which have resulted in the capture of Irles and the whole of our objectives, and of 280 prisoners, 15 machine-guns, and 4 trench mortars, with small casualties to ourselves.

Chapter 13

Impressions of a 'Push'

It has been said that marriages are made in Heaven, but bully beef and Maconochies are made in America, and offensives mostly in France.— Mudhook.

The preparations for an attack involve the whole-hearted co-operation of every branch of the Service, and its success largely depends upon the smooth co-ordination between each of these branches. The artillery arrange a barrage time-table and an adequate supply of ammunition; the trench mortars and machine-guns conform to this time-table, and in addition are prepared to move forward as required; the engineers lay mines, and at the psychological moment explode them; the Army Service Corps provide the necessary food and the battalion transports take it up to the new positions as soon as circumstances will allow; the medical services select suitable aid posts, and clear the battlefield of wounded; the pioneer battalions are in readiness to push roads forward in the back areas and to dig trenches during the consolidation of the objectives; and lastly, the infantry have to understand what is expected of them, and at 'zero' commence their advance.

It is only proposed here to indicate the medical preparations, and only these in the actual fighting zone will be described at any length.

Before a battalion takes over a portion of the line with a view to an attack, it is usual for the commanding officer, company commanders, and medical officer to visit the sector and gain what information they can, both from the occupants and from personal observation.

The commanding officer then issues a secret operation order, giving details as to the time and method of relief, and the disposition of the companies. In addition, an officers' conference is held at Battalion Headquarters, at which any obscure points are cleared up and the mode of attack is explained.

Secret orders are also issued to all medical officers by the A.D.M.S. (assistant director of medical services) of the division, explaining the arrangements for the evacuation of wounded.

The points of interest to the battalion medical officer are the situations of his primary aid post, the advanced dressing-station of the field ambulance, and the collecting point for walking wounded. He must also know the location of the advanced relay posts and bearer sub-divisions, whose duty it is to evacuate wounded from the regimental aid post. In addition, he must fully understand the position and nature of the objectives aimed at, in order to formulate a rough plan as to when he will advance his aid post and to what position.

Numerous other things must be carefully attended to. It must be ensured that every man in the battalion is in possession of a first field dressing. The medical personnel cannot carry a large supply of dressings, and so the covering of a man's wound may be dependent on his possessing a first field dressing.

Each battalion has eight stretchers. These have to be carefully examined to see that they are in perfect working order, and arrangements must be made that the bearer sub-division of the field ambulance can supply many more when required. An adequate supply of first field and shell dressings must be served out to all stretcher-bearers and medical unit ratings.

The importance of every man thoroughly applying whale oil to his feet before going up to the trenches, must be impressed on all company and platoon commanders. It undoubtedly has the effect of greatly diminishing the number of cases of so-called 'trench feet.'

My own kit for an attack consists of hypodermic syringe, a bottle of morphia solution, two water bottles—one full of brandy, the other of water—a haversack containing shell dressings, tourniquets, and a few instruments, and an abundant supply of cigarettes.

The duties of the medical officer are practically the same as those adopted in the routine holding of trenches, and have been described in a previous chapter. The number of wounded, however, which pass through his hands is so great that his methods of treatment have to be modified, and he has mainly to concentrate his attention on quick evacuation to the advanced dressing station of the field ambulance. The prime object of a battalion is to fight. Everything which will impair its efficiency must be sacrificed, and all is subservient to the exigencies of the service. This is the reason why quick evacuation of wounded from the battlefield is essential. The battalion medical officer collects the wounded in as sheltered spots as he can find. The ambulance bearer sub-division evacuates them by stretcher to the advanced dressing station of the field ambulance, whence they are sent on by motor ambulance to the main dressing station of the field ambulance, and then to the casualty clearing station, and from there they are despatched in hospital trains to the base hospitals.

In all actions there are a large number of 'walking wounded' cases. These are directed to make their way to a collecting point from where they are sent by motor lorry, G.S. wagon, or other transport to the railhead, and thence to hospital.

As the supply of stretcher squads is not inexhaustible, every man who can possibly walk to this collecting point is made to do so. Many who appear quite exhausted are able to walk slowly down after having a cigarette and a tot of brandy. This is the reason why I invariably carry a supply of both.

Over the page is given a diagrammatic sketch of the lines of evacuation of wounded during an attack:

As it is absolutely essential for the battalion medical officer to keep in close touch with the attacking companies, he, at the earliest possible moment, moves his aid post forward to a captured dugout, or if such is not available selects a suitable shell-hole, and marks it with a Red Cross flag so that his stretcher-bearers and walking wounded can find him. He sends the position of his new headquarters to the advanced dressing station, whose duty it is to keep in touch with him and evacuate his wounded back.

Such is a short description of some of the preparations we doctors have to make. Let us now imagine that all is ready, and in a few minutes the great 'push' is going to commence. Dawn is just breaking and a thick mist envelops everything. The companies are all on their jumping-off trenches waiting for 'zero' time to arrive. Officers are standing, watch in hand, ready for the fateful minute, non-commissioned officers are encouraging their platoons and giving final directions, and the men—from their cheery appearance it might well be thought they were going for a picnic, and indeed such is the term many of them apply to such an affair as the present. The commanding officer, adjutant, and medical officer are in a trench a short distance behind. 'Zero' time arrives. *Bang-bang—bang-bang-bang—bang-bang*, go the field guns; *Crrr-ump—crrr-ump* go the howitzers; shrapnel bursts overhead and machine-gun bullets whizz past. Hell seems to be let

EN ROUTE FOR THE FIELD AMBULANCE

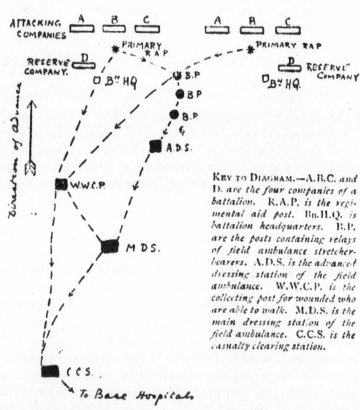

KEY TO DIAGRAM.—A.B.C. and D. are the four companies of a battalion. R.A.P. is the regimental aid post. Bn.H.Q. is battalion headquarters. B.P. are the posts containing relays of field ambulance stretcher-bearers. A.D.S. is the advanced dressing station of the field ambulance. W.W.C.P. is the collecting post for wounded who are able to walk. M.D.S. is the main dressing station of the field ambulance. C.C.S. is the casualty clearing station.

DIAGRAM OF EVACUATION OF WOUNDED

loose on the countryside.

The artillery have formed a barrage, under cover of which the infantry advance on the enemy trenches. The barrage slowly creeps forward; our men unconcernedly follow it. Up go the Boches' S.O.S. rockets until the scene resembles a Crystal Palace Brock's Benefit Night. The enemy artillery quickly reply to the frantic signals of their infantry, and *their* barrage opens. Many of our men fall—some dead, others wounded. The remainder push on and are in the Huns' front line directly our barrage has passed over it. Then bombing of dugouts and hand-to-hand fighting ensues. Many of our men fall, but few of them before doing all—or even more than all—that is expected of them.

The scene in 'No Man's Land' is indescribable. The ground is a mass of shell craters and almost impassable. The cries of the maimed and dying mingle strangely with the shriek of our own shells overhead and the explosions of hostile shells around us. That period of waiting—sufficient to try the hardest—is now over. The medical officer has his time fully occupied injecting morphia into the badly wounded, whilst his orderly affixes tallies marked with the dosage. Shell dressings and first field dressings are quickly applied, and the wounded are collected into groups in any spot which affords some shelter from the shells which are bursting around. The ambulance-bearers now arrive, and carry the cases back to their advanced dressing station.

The battalion medical personnel has to push on so as to keep in touch with the battalion, but on the way numerous cases are hastily treated and got into cover.

Large batches of prisoners are now beginning to come across 'No Man's Land.' These are at once commandeered to carry wounded back. Most of them appear only too willing to do so; those who object are quickly shown the error of their ways.

On getting into the German trenches it is exceedingly useful if a German aid post can be located and taken over. A Red Cross flag is stuck into the ground over it, to indicate the position of the medical officer to walking wounded and stretcher-bearers. On entering the aid post it is usual to find that the German medical officer has remained behind with his wounded. On one occasion I had three Boche doctors, in different dugouts, working under me. The German doctors are very different from their combatant brethren. I have found that they treat all wounded, regardless of their nationality. They are doctors first, and Boches a long way afterwards.

133

The next procedure is to collect all further wounded into this aid post or other place of comparative safety, from where they can be evacuated later by the field ambulance bearers.

The battalion has now reached its final objective, and the medical personnel, having collected all wounded, joins it in the new line which is being dug.

Suddenly the enemy open a furious barrage. Large numbers are seen congregating in front of us. They are advancing to counter-attack and drive us out of our new positions. Our artillery liaison officer quickly telephones back to his batteries. We open fire with machine-guns, Lewis guns, and rifles, and await events. There are a few minutes of suspense and then our deadly artillery barrage opens. The advancing line is seen to be greatly thinned, it wavers, and the remainder then ignominiously take to their heels. Our barrage lifts slightly and catches that remainder. The night is spent in consolidating the new line and repelling further counter-attacks.

A MODE OF PROTECTION AGAINST SHELL-FIRE

FRANCE—JUNE 1917

63RD (R.N.) DIVISION

(MAJOR-GENERAL LAWRIE)

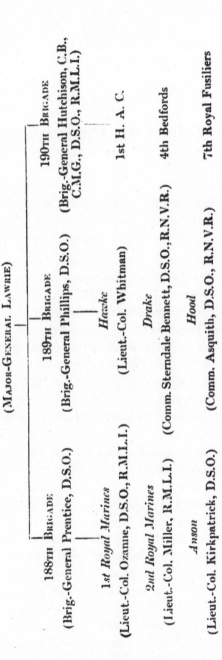

188TH BRIGADE
(Brig.-General Prentice, D.S.O.)

1st Royal Marines
(Lieut.-Col. Ozanne, D.S.O., R.M.L.I.)

2nd Royal Marines
(Lieut.-Col. Miller, R.M.L.I.)

Anson
(Lieut.-Col. Kirkpatrick, D.S.O.)

Howe
(Comm. West, D.S.O., R.N.V.R.)

189TH BRIGADE
(Brig.-General Phillips, D.S.O.)

Hawke
(Lieut.-Col. Whitman)

Drake
(Comm. Sterndale Bennett, D.S.O., R.N.V.R.)

Hood
(Comm. Asquith, D.S.O., R.N.V.R.)

Nelson
(Lieut.-Col. Lewis, D.S.O.)

190TH BRIGADE
(Brig.-General Hutchison, C.B.,
C.M.G., D.S.O., R.M.L.I.)

1st H. A. C.

4th Bedfords

7th Royal Fusiliers

10th Dublin Fusiliers

CHAPTER 14

Gavrelle and Passchendaele

It is not the length of existence which counts, but what is achieved during that existence, however short.
        —W, G. C. Gladstone in a letter to his mother.

Where there is a big offensive, there also will the R.N.D. be found, is now regarded as almost a platitude, and hence it caused us no surprise whatever, when early in April 1917 the division was ordered to entrain for Aubigne, a little country town in the vicinity of Arras. The attack had been launched in this sector from Givenchy-en-Gohelle to Croisilles on April 9th, and before our arrival the following places had been captured—Tilloy, St. Martin-sur-Cojeul, St. Laurent Blangy, Athies, Fampoux, Héninal, Monchy-le-Preux, Wancourt, Givenchy-en-Gohelle, Vimy, Willerval, and Bailleul.

On April 16th the French attacked on the Aisne. They did not meet with the success which was anticipated, and hence, as a diversion, to distract the enemy from our ally's front, it was decided to continue our advance in the direction of Douai and Cambrai, by attacking on a nine-mile front from Gavrelle to Croisilles. The northern part of this sector stretches from Gavrelle, over the Arras-Douai railway to Roeux and the River Scarpe. The village of Gavrelle lies on the Arras-Douai road and further along this high road is Fresnes. The fact that Vimy Ridge was now in our hands was an effective barrier to the Germans reinforcing Gavrelle from Oppy and Fresnoy, as the intervening country was in consequence commanded by our artillery fire.

On April 22nd, the 188th Brigade (1st and 2nd Royal Marines, Anson, and Howe Battalions) took up its position in what had on April 9th been the original German front line system of trenches. They were in support to the 189th Brigade (Hawke, Drake, Hood,

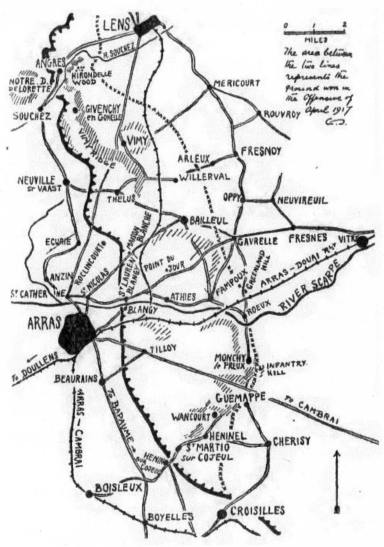

MILES

The area between
the two lines
represents the
ground won in
the Offensive of
April 1917
G.J.

LENS
ANGRES
H. SOUCHEZ
NOTRE. D.
DE LORETTE
HIRONDELLE
WOOD
SOUCHEZ
GIVENCHY
en GONELLE
MERICOURT
ROUVROY
VIMY
ARLEUX
FRESNOY
NEUVILLE
St VAAST
WILLERVAL
THELUS
OPPY
NEUVIREUIL
VIMY RIDGE
ECURIE
MAISON BLANCHE
BAILLEUL
GAVRELLE
FRESNES
VITRY
ANZIN
ROCLINCOURT
St NICOLAS
St LAURENT
BLANGY
POINT DU
JOUR
FAMPOUX
GREENLAND
HILL
ARRAS—DOUAI Rly
St CATHERINE
ATHIES
ROEUX
RIVER SCARPE
ARRAS
BLANGY
TILLOY
To DOULLENS
MONCHY
le PREUX
INFANTRY
HILL
BEAURAINS
To CAMBRAI
GUEMAPPE
ARRAS—CAMBRAI
To BAPAUME
WANCOURT
HENINEL
St MARTIO
sur COJEUL
CHERISY
HENIN
sur COJEUL
BOISLEUX
BOYELLES
CROISILLES
ARRAS—CAMBRAI

MAP OF THE ARRAS ADVANCE

and Nelson Battalions) which, along with various English and Scottish brigades, was to attack on the morrow.

At 4.45 a.m. on St. George's Day, 1917, our barrage lifted slightly, and the attack along the whole nine-mile front commenced. The Royal Naval Division advanced on Gavrelle, and before 9 a.m. this strongly fortified village was in our hands, mainly due to the superb leadership and great personal gallantry of Commander Arthur Asquith, D.S.O., R.N.V.R. Simultaneously the troops on our right captured Guémappe, Infantry Hill, the high ground west of Chérisy, Greenland Hill, and the outskirts of Roeux.

The enemy repeatedly counter-attacked in great strength. The Royal Naval Division alone successfully resisted seven counter-attacks on Gavrelle, on every occasion driving back the enemy, who charged up the Arras-Douai road from Fresnes, with enormous slaughter. Only once did the Germans force us to evacuate the ruins, but their success was short-lived, and they were soon ejected at the point of the bayonet. By the end of the engagement, five hundred prisoners, including seventeen officers, were in our hands, and in addition, line upon line of grey-clad German corpses were strewn on the plain betwixt Gavrelle and Fresnes—an eloquent testimony to the costliness of their determined counter-attacks, and to the effectiveness of our rifle and machine-gun fire.

In connection with this attack, the following appreciative message was received from Major-General Lawrie:

SPECIAL ORDER OF THE DAY ISSUED BY THE G.O.C. 63RD
(R.N.) DIVISION, APRIL 24, 1917

The Divisional Commander wishes to place on record his admiration of the magnificent work of the division in the recent operations. As in the case of the Battle of the Ancre, the division was entrusted with a most difficult and important task, and once more it has completely justified the trust reposed in it and has added still further to its great traditions. The infantry not only succeeded in capturing the whole of an important and strongly defended village on the flank of the army's attack, but they withstood unshaken the heavy artillery fire which was directed on them during the whole period of consolidation, and successfully beat off no fewer than seven counter-attacks.

On the night of April 24th, the 188th Brigade relieved the 189th Brigade in the newly captured trenches near the village of Gavrelle.

.....Some sepulchred Gavrelle

Some shattered homes in their own dust concealed

During the following few days we were subjected to a very heavy and accurate fire, and of necessity suffered many casualties. On the night of April 26th a small party of Royal Marines, under Lieutenant Markham, attempted to advance slightly our front line, but met with severe resistance and suffered many casualties, including their gallant leader, who died a soldier's death, fighting bravely to the end.

It was now apparent that in order to hold our positions another attack was necessary, and hence orders were issued to advance the line both north and south of Gavrelle over an eight-mile front. On April 28th, 1917, at 4.25 a.m. the 188th Brigade, with British troops on their left and Canadians on their right, attacked. A strong opposition was met with, but to our north ground was gained at Arleux-en-Gohelle and Oppy, whilst to our south the line was advanced near Roeux and Monchy.

As far as the Royal Naval Division was concerned, the main feature of this attack was the capture and defence of the famous mill of Gavrelle. One platoon of Royal Marines, under the command of Lieutenant George Newling, was told off to take this important stronghold. After breaking through a very strong defence line, they stormed the windmill at the point of the bayonet. The enemy counter-attacked strongly and gained the edge of the village, entirely cutting off the mill from our line. Thirteen attacks were made on the village, each one sweeping over the remains of the now nearly demolished mill, but the gallant little garrison still held out in spite of the fact that they were without food or water, and their ammunition was well-nigh exhausted. At last the enemy desisted from his costly counter-attacks, and the post was relieved and reinforced.

Thirty Marines came out of it, including their commander and Major Eagles, the latter of whom had managed during the night to reach the point and assist in its defence. (Major Eagles, who gained his D.S.O. for magnificent work in Gallipoli, was killed just one year later leading his company of Marines at the Zeebrugge landing on St. George's Day, 1918.) On April 30th we were relieved by the West Yorks and went back into camp, leaving behind in 'sepulchred Gavrelle' many gallant comrades who had so bravely upheld the honour of the Royal Naval Division and enhanced its reputation to such an extent that from henceforth it ranked as one of the finest *fighting* divisions of the British Army.

On the following morning we marched back by easy stages, and early in May settled down in rest billets, where a busy week was spent reforming the Division.

On May 12th, 1917, we returned to the Arras sector and went into camp. The next few months were spent holding trenches in the vicinity of Gavrelle, and nothing of note occurred beyond numerous successful raids in which the Anson and Howe Battalions played a prominent part. Regarding our work here, it is only necessary to quote a letter received by the Divisional Commander from Lieutenant-General Sir W. N. Congreve, V.C., who commanded the corps:

To G.O.C. 63rd (R.N.) Division
From inspection and examination of photographs I gather that your Division has dug during its late tour in the trenches as well as it fought in the capture of Gavrelle. Please convey to all ranks my satisfaction and thanks.

W. N. Congreve, Lt.-General,
Commanding —— Corps.
10th June 1917.

General Congreve very frequently visited our trenches, and it was during one of these visits that he was so severely wounded. The wonderful coolness under shell-fire, the kindly interest and the strong common sense of this distinguished and very gallant officer greatly endeared him to all ranks of the Royal Naval Division, and we felt we had lost not only a fine commander, but also a friend who appreciated our difficulties and alleviated our hardships in every way which the exigencies of the service would permit.

When out of the line, many pleasant hours were spent in Arras, that fine old cathedral town which, being situated just behind our lines, was partially destroyed, but still remained a noble ruin and boasted of a very comfortable officers' club, most efficiently managed by the Expeditionary Force Canteen. Here the officers of the Royal Naval Division frequently forgathered, and its name conjures up memories of many pleasant dinners with friends who are now no more.

A certain little village where we were frequently billeted is affectionately remembered by many of us as one of the most comfortable resting-places on the western front. The inhabitants showed us kindnesses too numerous to mention, too sincere to be ever forgotten. It was here that the R.M.L.H. (Royal Marine Light Horse) was formed—a purely unofficial little band, with Lieutenant-Colonel Wainwright as commanding officer, whose function was to explore, on pleasure bent, the surrounding country when out of the line. Many were the gallops we had across country, and after a pleasant dinner of the omelet and champagne variety at some little estaminet, the return journey in the cool of the evening. Such little episodes as these were largely responsible for the unfailing good humour and bonhomie of the Royal Marine battalions, which rendered them so popular with all units with whom they had any dealings-official or otherwise.

On June 19th, Admiral of the Fleet Lord Charles Beresford inspected the division. This fine old sailor walked through the ranks, every now and then stopping to chat with some old Marine he recognised as having served in his fleet in the old days. The rousing cheers which greeted him were ample proof of the esteem in which he was held by all. Lieutenant-Colonel Miller has since told me that from a military standpoint, the most amazing episode of this inspection was the conduct of a little group of officers with whom Lord Charles paused awhile to talk. First came the strictly Service quartermaster, fully appreciating all that was due to an Admiral of the Fleet, next the doctor, somewhat embarrassed and nervous, then the chaplain who, with arms *akimbo* and a broad grin on his boyish face, took the greatest interest in the proceedings, but forgot to salute, and lastly, the cosmopolitan little French interpreter, who shook hands warmly with his right hand, vainly attempting to conceal an enormous cigar of dreadful odour in his left.

On July 9th, the King inspected that part of the Royal Naval Division which was not in the trenches, but, as I was then sitting disconsolately in a very wet dugout in the front line, I am unable to give any details of the event, though it was very greatly appreciated by all who were present.

On September 18th, 1917, the division left the Arras sector, and after a short rest, on October 2nd entrained for Hopoutre and went into camp near Poperinghe to act as a reserve for the attack of October 4th. This attack being successfully accomplished, we were taken by motor buses back to rest billets.

About this time the collapse of Russia quite negatived any hope of the British advancing from Passchendaele against the German line of communication with Ostend and Zeebrugge, but it was essential to continue the attack in order to contain a large number of enemy troops in this region, which otherwise might be sent to Italy to press home the unexpected defeats sustained by General Cadorna's forces. It was decided that the Royal Naval Division should attack on October 26th, and until this date we remained at Hertzeele training hard.

Our Interpreter

'Le Lion Blanc'

There were few relaxations here, and my only pleasant memory of the village was the excellent dinners served in the '*Lion Blanc*,' a comfortable *estaminet*, presided over by the inimitable Lulu, where the men also were able to spend many happy hours in the low long room on the ground floor.

Over this little village of Hertzeele in the back areas the sun was fitfully gleaming through the clouds, as one day riding through the sea of mud I suddenly came upon 'A' Company of the 2nd Royal Marines, and paused a moment to listen. Their commanding officer. Captain Ligertwood, was telling them that in a few days they were going over the top, and that in the attack he wished each platoon to carry a flag which would serve as a rallying point, and like the regimental colours of old, inspire the men.

These flags, each consisting of only a strip of red canvas nailed to a stick cut from the adjoining woods, were solemnly blessed by Father Davey, the battalion chaplain, and handed to each of the four platoons. The men regarded them as sacred, and when some few days later they went over the top, these makeshift flags served the purpose for which they were intended.

In the attack Captain Ligertwood, thrice wounded, still led on his depleted company, but his fourth wound was so severe as to prevent him walking further. Lying in that sea of mud, swept by machine-gun and rifle fire, he made a supreme effort, struggled painfully to his feet, pointed to the objective and said, 'There's your objective, lads, get it!' The exertion was too much for his quickly ebbing strength and soon he died, and by the manner of his death added a fresh leaf to the proud laurel wreath of the Royal Marines, and left behind a memory of the 'honour, courage, and loyalty' which is so intimately associated with the name of his fine old corps.

Some months later. Lieutenant Hore brought home one of these tattered, weather-stained flags to Plymouth, and at a ceremonial parade it was handed over to the Plymouth Division of the Royal Marines in memory of the gallant stand made by 'A' Company, during the latter phases of the Passchendaele attack.

On October 23rd, 1917, the Royal Naval Division returned to the canal bank near Ypres, in readiness for the attack. October 24th and 25th were fine, but intensely cold, and early on October 26th a torrential downpour commenced, which converted the marshy, low-lying ground round Ypres into veritable quagmires, which were almost impassable. The 188th Brigade of the Royal Naval Division, in conjunction with a Canadian division, at dawn on the cold, wet morning of October 26th, commenced to advance through the sea of mud on the innumerable redoubts and pill-boxes between the Lekkebotte-beek and the south of Passchendaele, whilst Lancashire troops attacked on Polderhoek Château and Gheluvelt.

The Royal Marines, Howe, and Anson Battalions gallantly plod-ded through the waist-deep mud under a withering machine-gun and rifle fire, along the banks of the Paddebeek, down the slopes of the Wallemolen spur in the direction of Goudberg and Passchendaele. From countless pill-boxes and redoubts bullets rained like hail on our dauntless men, but many of these strongholds were captured at the point of the bayonet or by bombing attacks.

My further recollections of this gallant fight are somewhat mixed, as, owing to circumstances over which I had no control, on the after-noon of October 26th I found myself being conveyed back to field ambulance. However, no tributes could be more worthy of the fine conduct of the Royal Naval Division than the following appreciative messages:

From General Gough, October 26, 1917

> Please convey to all ranks engaged in today's operations my very great appreciation of their gallant efforts. They have my sincere sympathy, as no troops could have had to face worse conditions of mud than they had to face owing to the sudden downfall of rain this morning. No troops could have done more than our men did today, and, given a fair chance, I have every confidence in their complete success every time.

From Commander-in-Chief, October 27, 1917

> Please assure all troops engaged that I thoroughly appreci-ate their fine effort yesterday under the terrible conditions of ground and weather. The ground gained by the division is of great importance, and the determined fighting of other divi-sions contributed in no small degree to the important success achieved on the main ridge.

From General Gough, October 31, 1917

> Please convey to the officers and men engaged in yesterday's operations my thanks and great appreciation for their gallant efforts. Nothing but the impossibility of crossing the mud pre-vented their usual complete success.

From General Plumer, November 4, 1917

Very glad Division got Sourd Farm last night.

A PILL-BOX AT PASSCHENDAELE

CHAPTER 15

The Psychology of the Soldier

We don't get much moneys but we do see Life.

Thomas Atkins.

A study of the psychology of the soldier is an absorbingly inter-esting, but at the same time an extremely difficult subject . In the muddy trenches of France, where death is ever lurking, where the end is so sudden and the summons to the unknown so rapid, where you pass a cheery word with your dearest friend one hour, and the next meet his mangled body being carried down the communication trench to the battalion burying ground; where these things exist the soldier mainly lives for the present and only seldom attempts to look into the future. He soon becomes inured to the gruesome sight of a shattered form and a blood-stained firestep, but the haunting thought sooner or later enters his brain that someday *his* blood will stain the firestep, *his* mangled body block the trench, *his* wife be a widow, and *his* children fatherless. It is the personal element, the primeval trait of self-preservation, which becomes abnormally developed when sitting inactively in a front line trench, subjected to a heavy barrage.

I have studied the soldier in many phases—in the attack with the blood-lust gleaming in his eye, in the routine holding of trenches waiting for a counter-attack, in the back areas trying to avoid an irk-some fatigue, in the divisional cinema laughing like a schoolboy, in the estaminet clamouring for his beer, in his home life surrounded by his children, and I have sat with him as he laboriously breathed his last and passed into that great Beyond, where there are no bar-rages and no fatigues, but all is peace. Each phase gives a new insight into his complex character, and the sum total is that I find him almost unfathomable.

Let us follow him step by step through the various stages of an attack. First we see him sitting in his ruined billet a few miles behind the line, waiting for orders to move up to the trenches, and spending his time writing a few lines to his wife in 'Blighty.' Looking over his shoulder we read the last sentence of his letter, which runs ' ... Doant be anxious deer if you doant get another letter for some days. Hopping this finds you in the pink as it leaves me at present, Your affect, hubbie Alf.' What pathos and tragedy are in this ill-spelt sentence! None knows better than the author of it how slender his chances of ever writing another letter are, but still he never was a demonstrative man, and he is rather ashamed of the emotion he experiences when he thinks he may never see her again, and after all, he meditates, why should he trouble her with his fears, which are probably only the figment of an over-active imagination—has she not sufficient worries without his adding to them?

Next we see him struggling up that interminable communication trench to the front line—cheerily tramping along, his shoulders aching with their heavy burden, knee deep in the clayey mud, but full of the joys of the morrow when he is going to meet the Boche face to face, and show his adversary how infinitely superior the British Tommy is to the German automaton.

At midnight we find him in the front line waiting for 'zero' hour to arrive. This is the most trying period of his whole existence. He is going over the top at dawn—possibly to his death. He is not afraid of dying, and has no doubt in his own mind but that when the time comes he will do his duty. It is this awful suspense of waiting for dawn which he thinks will soon drive him mad. He has a paroxysmal attack of the most abject fear, but yet he is no coward. He masters this fear and lies down on the firestep to get a few hours' rest, but sleep will not come. His mind seems preternaturally clear and he remembers trivial incidents long since forgotten. How he longs for dawn! You, my masters, who live comfortably at home—your only experience of war a puny air raid—cannot realise the terrible tension of waiting for 'zero.' Next time you see the dawn breaking over a peaceful and prosperous England, remember that somewhere in France it may be zero hour, and the men may be struggling across 'No Man's Land,' giving their lives that you and such as you may continue to live in peace and prosperity. Remember zero hour and try to picture what it means, and then go down on your knees and thank God for giving you the finest man the world has ever seen—the British Tommy.

Word is passed along to stand by, and a minute later our barrage opens with a deafening roar. The time is come. All the fears and forebodings of that dreadful wait are swept aside. He becomes alert and watchful, and scrambling out of the trench with the rest of his platoon, plods gallantly across that intervening hell, swept by a hail of shrapnel and high explosives from the ever-watchful enemy guns. Suddenly he feels a burning sensation in his leg—knows it is badly shattered—finds he can walk no longer, and pitches head-first into a shell-hole. Here he is found by the stretcher-bearers, still cheerful and uncomplaining, bearing the torture of his wound with the fortitude with which he has borne all his previous trials. The medical officer sees at a glance that his case is hopeless, and all that can be done is to render his passage into eternity as painless as possible. And so, lying in a muddy shell-hole somewhere in France, he breathes his last. Weeks later his name appears in the casualty list. Do you, my readers, as you sit at your comfortable breakfast-table, casually glancing through this list of killed, realise the pathos which is attached to every name. Remember sometimes that each one of these knew that he was probably going to his death, but went cheerfully, so that *you* might continue your placid existence untroubled by the awful tragedy of war in England.

The attack has been successful, and on the following night we are relieved. The battalion, now so pathetically diminished in numbers, wends its weary way back to billets. The men, though tired, footsore, lousy, unshaven, and caked with mud from head to foot, are remarkably cheery. The last two days are a thing of the past, and hence forgotten. They live for the present, and the thought uppermost in every man's mind is that their efficient quartermaster will have a tot of rum for each one of them on their return to billets. This expectation is realised, and wrapping themselves up in their blankets, they are soon enjoying a well-earned night's repose.

On the following day, sitting in a partially demolished village just behind the trenches, I attempt to fathom the mysteries of the British soldier's nature, and fail miserably in the attempt. How curious it seems that these cheery, high-spirited fellows, sitting in the local *estaminets*, each with his glass of innocuous '*vinne blank*,' puffing perseveringly at the inevitable woodbine, and making amorous advances to the delightful French girls, were only yesterday face to face with a very imminent death, and have by their reckless devotion to duty added a fresh lustre to the traditions of their already famous division!

The psychology of the soldier is truly beyond the comprehen-

THE APPLIANCES OF MODERN WARFARE

HELPING MADEMOISELLE TO DRAW WATER
FROM THE WELL

sion of most of us. They ruthlessly kill Boches, and endure the mental agony of being face to face with almost certain death, but still on the following night these hardened warriors, the tragedy of it all forgotten, are found sitting in the divisional cinema, shrieking with laughter over the ridiculous antics of their prime favourite, Charlie Chaplin.

They never complain, but still each man has his 'grouse.' 'Calls us blooming light infantry, they does; I feels more like a Christmas-tree,' ironically soliloquises an old soldier, manfully staggering along, carrying the innumerable appliances of modern warfare. Call digging a 'fatigue' and the 'grouse' becomes pronounced; call it a 'working party,' and there is hardly a murmur. Tell them they are going 'over the top' tomorrow, and no man, however ill he may feel, reports sick. Suggest a long day's route march in the back area, and many develop strange and awful complaints quite unknown to the medical faculty. 'I eats well and I drinks well and I takes my rum hearty, but as soon as I hears of this 'ere march I feels all over alike,' is how the patient describes his symptoms. The prescription of 'One No. 9 pill three times daily until cured' is the polite way in which the hard-hearted medical officer tactfully informs his would-be patient that his ailment is purely imaginary. This remedy has a remarkably efficacious effect.

On one occasion, adopting a very lowly attitude, I made a strategical advance to see a wounded man lying in the open. I found him nursing a badly fractured jaw and having, in addition, numerous other wounds. He did not complain of his pain; he never mentioned the shell-fire or cold; he did not even ask if the wound was likely to be fatal. His only question was, 'Is my false teeth all right, sir? I paid two-thirteen-nine for them at Goldstein's just afore war.' The assurance that his lower denture was intact had a remarkably sedative effect on him, and undoubtedly increased his chances of recovery.

In a recent operation, I found a man lying wounded in a shell-hole. 'Blighty one this time, sir,' he said cheerfully, doubtless thinking of the two previous occasions when he had been wounded and got no further than the casualty clearing station. He had a compound fracture of both legs, and died in the field ambulance on the following day.

'Don't waste time over me, doctor, I'm done in. There's plenty of others wanting you,' casually remarked a severe abdominal case on a very busy morning. All he would accept was a cigarette—he died peacefully ten minutes later, puffing contentedly until the end.

An officer came into my aid post one night with a man of his platoon who was suffering from a fractured leg. After the somewhat lengthy operation of immobilising the fracture between a rifle and a pick handle, I was somewhat surprised when the officer apologetically asked me to look at his eye, as he had got 'a bit of mud or something in it.' On examination it was obvious that his sight in that eye was irretrievably lost. He walked down to the field ambulance behind the stretcher bearing the man, encouraging him to stand the pain, and making light of his own much more serious injury.

A company sergeant-major had his arm blown off at the shoulder, but seeing his company commander approaching, drew himself up smartly to attention, apologised for ' being no more good,' and then collapsed in a heap on the ground.

Such incidents as these could be multiplied indefinitely, but they would only go to show the courage, endurance, unconscious humour and unfailing optimism of the soldier when confronted by the unutterable tragedy, suffering, and horror of a great war.

Back in rest billets we see much of the French. Both old and young are quite irresistible. The flapper who coyly calls a stern battalion commander '*un beaucoup, beaucoup, BEAUCOUP brigand*'; her mother, who christens the medical officer '*mon petit enfant*'; the little fellows who sell the *Daily Mail* in these ruined villages, shouting 'piper' in the most approved Fleet Street style; the girls who reply to our questions with an invariable '*après la guerre*,' or 'no *bon* for the troops'; the *poilu en permission* who gives us cunningly made *souvenirs de boche*; and the old man who unconcernedly ploughs the fields a few miles behind the firing line—all are typical of the French.

At first the insular Briton is somewhat surprised to find that they do not live entirely on a staple diet of frogs and sweet champagne, as we were so gravely assured in our schooldays. We find them an exceedingly temperate race, who eat what we eat and drink what we drink. They have the same amusements as we, most of our good qualities, and what binds us even more closely to them, a few of our failings. They possess all the attributes which we complacently *used* to consider peculiar to the British nation.

At first the common bond of friendship was the cause for which both nations were fighting. Now, in addition, there is the much more intimate bond of personal respect, admiration, and affection between individuals who have received kindnesses from one another which can never be forgotten, who have fought and died side by side, and who, as a result of the war, appreciate and honour one another.

The *camaraderie* between our now cosmopolitan soldiers and the blushing village maidens does more to cement the '*entente*' than the most eloquent speeches at Westminster.

The Tommy spends his off-duty hours helping *Mademoiselle* to draw water from the well, carrying her buckets home for her, feeding the cows, cleaning the farmyard, and helping her generally in his own inimitable style. He asks for no reward, but feels amply repaid if she deigns to accept his services, and allows him to bask in the sunshine of her smile. She, knowing instinctively he can be trusted, does her best to entertain him during the few days he is back in billets, and they finally part with mutual regrets.

The war has undoubtedly broadened the Briton's outlook on life. His patriotism is no longer the old Jingo patriotism of former days, but is a real and personal thing, entailing hardships and sacrifices hitherto undreamt of, and often even death—the supreme sacrifice of all.

JINGO-PATRIOTISM OF FORMER DAYS

CHAPTER 16

The Soldier's Ailments in France

Mens sana in corpore sano.

In these modern days, when Mrs. Brown unblushingly tells Mr. Smith about the idiosyncrasies of her digestive tract, and Major Jones's chief topic of conversation at breakfast is the state of his liver, whilst their young daughters discourse learnedly on the respective merits of gastro-enterostomy, appendicectomy, exploratory-laparotomy, and other complex surgical procedures, it may not be entirely out of place or wholly uninteresting to the reader if I briefly mention some of the diseases met with on active service.

LICE.

Ye ugly, creepin', blastit wonner.
Detested, shunn'd by saunt an' sinner.

A certain famous Oxford Don has described lice as one of *'the minor horrors of war.'* Most of us who have experienced the ravages of these little insects are more forcible and less polite in our description of the agony of mind and body which these ubiquitous parasites can cause.

Lice are always found where men are crowded together. They are not, as is popularly believed, the result of uncleanliness, but they always flourish best in dirty surroundings.

Going round the trenches on a fine day, it is customary to see every man who is off duty stripped to the waist, hunting in his shirt for these noxious insects, and viciously torturing them to death between his finger-nails.

To be bombarded heavily by hostile artillery is bad, to contract lice is worse, but a combination of the two is the very acme of discomfort and enough to make even a phlegmatic Scotsman seriously contemplate suicide. They get into one's clothing, and wander all over the body, causing intense irritation—*toujours le promenade* as the polite French say. Sleep is impossible. The unfortunate victim lies awake scratching every portion of his anatomy until he is finally a mass of bleeding excoriations. In addition, it must be remembered that typhus fever, relapsing fever, and trench fever are all carried from man to man by lice.

On one occasion I was credibly informed that a certain platoon commander of my acquaintance caught forty-two on his trousers alone in the space of one short hour, and that his company commander had been even more successful in his researches.

This is, I know, an unsavoury subject, but it is one of paramount importance to those affected. That such a condition exists is hardly realised and never talked of by those at home, but it is one which is deserving of the greatest sympathy. No absolutely certain method of prevention has yet been discovered, though many have been tried with varying success. The inventor of a true preventive would gain the undying gratitude of countless sufferers.

Once lice have been contracted, they are exceedingly difficult to get rid of.

They say that a dear little wife
Will stick to one even thro' Hell,
But I'm sure she couldn't stick closer
Than those lice I picked up at Gavrelle,

is how the condition was aptly described by a friend of mine.

De-lousing stations are now established all over France, (as at time of first publication), and they deal very efficiently with men as soon as they come out of the trenches. In addition, Oxford Powder, a strong insecticide, is served out to men before going up to the trenches, and medical officers give frequent lectures on all known methods of combating the disease.

SHELL SHOCK.

Everyone has heard of the term 'shell shock,' many know some of the unfortunate victims of this distressing malady, but it is only the trench workers who have actually seen how it is produced. The word, as used by the laity, is very indefinite and covers a multitude of diseases, ranging in severity from temporary fear to a serious nervous condition.

155

From a medical standpoint, true shell shock is partly mental and partly physical in origin. It is caused by being in close proximity to a bursting projectile of high calibre. The man is practically always blown over by the rush of the shell, and when it bursts is buried by the debris and deafened by the explosion. He may or may not be wounded. What actually produces the condition is that a temporary vacuum is formed around him, which is rapidly filled by a great rush of air, causing a transitory increase of atmospheric pressure in his immediate vicinity.

The brain is an exceedingly delicate structure, surrounded by cerebro-spinal fluid, whose function is to protect it from outside influences. Any sudden severe change in the atmospheric pressure causes a disturbance in the cerebro-spinal fluid, and hence may produce an injury to the under-lying cerebral tissue.

Shell shock is one of the most distressing complaints it is possible to witness. A man who yesterday was full of intellect and vitality, quick in decision, a charming companion, a trusted friend and an efficient soldier, is today an entirely different person, with twitching hands, apathetic eye, and full of that curious indecision which in peace time we associated with a defect of the higher mental centres. Most cases are curable, but the condition is apt to recur when the individual is subjected to a similar shock.

Many officers and men are invalided home suffering from shell shock, and it must be clearly understood that such persons before the particular incident which caused their present condition were, as a rule, not neurotic individuals. The majority of such cases are men who have always done their duty, often in the face of almost certain death, and many of them have gained our most coveted decorations.

Shell shock must not be confused with that equally interesting condition called by Huot of the French Medical Service 'le Cafard,' which is merely a nervous debility that attacks men after long spells in the trenches under trying conditions.

I mentioned that, though mainly physical, shell shock was also partly mental in origin. By this I mean that the more highly educated a man is, the more likely he is to be affected by an explosion in his immediate vicinity. A somewhat apt analogy is that of a man who wishes a tooth extracted when no anaesthetic is available. The pain of such a procedure is to a large extent mental, but still the coalheaver can stand it much better than the city clerk, and the hard-riding hunting man much better than the learned Oxford Don. It is not a question of courage, but of that extremely vague quantity known as temperament.

Nature is a mass of contradictions, or perhaps more accurately of compensations. Most normal individuals would walk a mile in order to escape a shelling, and yet there are some who appear to have a positive liking, or at least a profound indifference for the fiendish inventions of the Boche. I well remember my first introduction to the *Minnenwerfer*. Standing with a platoon in a front line trench, I suddenly saw a thousand pounds of high explosive wobbling unnaturally through the air towards us. I freely admit that a cold shudder ran down my spine, as I vaguely wondered what this devilish invention could be, but this feeling was quickly mingled with one of intense amusement when I heard an irrepressible Cockney remarking to his pal, 'Good Gawd, Bill, 'ere's 'alf Lens comin' over.' To most of us fear of the unknown is fear personified In a few days' time, when we knew these engines of death more intimately, we affectionately called them 'Minnies' or 'Rum Jars.'

The man who appears to have a sneaking affection for shells is said by his friends to have '*beaucoup guts*'—an expressive term, though savouring somewhat of the farmyard.

All men who have seen much active service are necessarily rather fatalists. After coming through one or two attacks unscathed, they develop a supreme contempt for all shells which do not hit them, and adopt the comfortable philosophy that until a shell is shoved into the breech with, metaphorically speaking, their name written upon it, they are safe from injury.

TRENCH DISEASES.

In the present war, three new diseases have appeared—trench feet, trench fever, and trench nephritis. We now know the causation of the first two, and so are able to take efficient measures to prevent their occurrence to any very large extent.

Trench fever is undoubtedly spread from man to man by lice, and I have already mentioned the methods we adopt to kill these pests.

Trench feet are prevented by rubbing whale oil into the feet, warm, clean socks, thigh boots when necessary, and, as far as possible, draining the trenches of surplus water.

Of the ordinary diseases of peace time, little need be said. In spite of the climatic conditions and great hardships of this present war, statistics clearly show that the percentage of sickness is much smaller in our Army in France than in the civil population at home.

In the South African War more men died from typhoid alone than from wounds; in the present war the number of deaths from this disease has been insignificant. This is partly due to inoculation, but chiefly to our wonderful sanitary arrangements. The scourges of previous campaigns—plague, cholera, and typhus—are quite unknown in France. They appeared in certain other theatres of war, but modern sanitary science quickly stamped them out.

HUNTING SCENE IN THE TRENCHES

CHAPTER 17

On Leave, Memories of France, and L'Envoi

A chiel's amang ye takin' notes,
And, faith, he'll prent it!
                                    Burns.

'Leave is a privilege, not a right,' quoted our regulation-bound adjutant in his most Service tones as, clicking my spurred heels together, I smartly saluted him and again asked if I were not nearly due for a 'drop o' Blighty.' The twinkle in his eye, however, aroused the suspicion in my mind that these stern words were mainly for the benefit of his orderly-room sergeant, who was vainly trying to conceal the emotion which my humble request evoked in his well-disciplined mind. Nor was I mistaken, for a few days later a breathless runner dashed into my medical inspection room with the message—'Please render to this office forthwith your address whilst on leave.'

Dinner that night was a joyous affair. The colonel, with the prospect of rehearsing the normal formation of attack at an early hour on the following morning, shortly retired to woo that fickle jade Morpheus, and left the major, adjutant, quartermaster, and transport officer—all of whom had promised to see me off for my train in the early hours of the morrow. We drew our chairs round the fire, each lit one of Wills's incomparable '*Trois Châteaux*,' filled our glasses to the brim, thanked God we were back in comfortable billets, and started to reminisce about home.

The transport officer told us of a delightful flapper he once met in the park and took to the movies, of the wonderful dinner they subsequently had in the Troc, and how, thanks to the excellent Cliquot, she had consented to adopt him as her 'lonely subaltern,' and now sent him weekly boxes of luxuries from home; the major enthused over a 'typewriter' he used to know in his wild subaltern days; the adjutant, married, of course, expressed his disapprobation of the friends of his brother officers; whilst the rubicund quartermaster suggested that 'another little drink wouldn't do us any harm.' And so the hours passed until the mess cart which was to take me to the station was announced. The adjutant then read to me the dire penalties of attempting to smuggle home shells, five-point nines, Boche rifles, uncensored letters, or other property belonging to the government, and to the shouts of 'Goodbyee-ee, Goodbyee-ee,' I set out on my journey. The less said of that dreary drive to the station, of my interview with the sleepy and none too polite railway transport officer, and the apparently never-ending journey to the base, the better. The only item of interest was watching the small French boys, who, apparently with no great exertion, raced the train for miles, begging us for souvenirs, bully beef, and suchlike commodities dear to the heart of the gamin.

Eventually we reached the coast and I made my way to the leave boat, where everything was bustle and full of interest. The M.L.O., resplendent in blue tabs, enormous spurs, an exquisite hunting stock, and carrying a murderous-looking trench stick heavily weighted with lead, scrutinised our leave warrants and marshalled us over the narrow gangway on board. The number of betabbed officers, red, blue, black, and green, gave quite a tone to the somewhat dingy vessel, and caused the muddy, unkempt trench-worker to become very conscious of the many deficiencies in his sartorial equipment. At last we were off. A brigadier, setting his hat at the approved nautical angle, climbed up on the bridge beside the skipper, but unfortunately *mal-de-mer* claimed him for her own, and, with a haste rarely seen in one of his exalted rank, he rushed below.

Why, I dreamily wondered, do mechanical transport officers invariably wear spurs, why are A.S.C. officials usually replete with revolvers and other warlike apparatus which they are so rarely called on to use, and why does every staff officer of field rank, as soon as he is in sight of England's shores surreptitiously change his khaki headgear for a wondrous affair, resplendent with red and gold and patent leather peak?

The leave train majestically steamed into Victoria. A prehistoric porter of venerable appearance kindly consented to look after my scanty belongings, and I hastened up the platform to change my French money into John Bradburys, cunningly avoiding *en route* an officious-looking Ak Pip Emma (known in England, I later discov-

THE M.L.O.

A porter of prehistoric
appearance.

A PORTER OF PREHISTORIC APPEARANCE

ered, as a Hay Pea Hem), who was apparently chasing young officers who had carelessly left their gloves and walking-sticks in the trenches, or whose *putties* and clothes had been somewhat torn on the German wire during the attack a few days previously. By dint of grossly over-tipping numerous ragged urchins, I eventually obtained a taxi, and directing the driver to the G—— Hotel I sank luxuriously on to the cushions and wondered if dear old London had altered much since I last visited her. Arriving at the hotel where I had frequently stayed in the piping days of peace, I was somewhat brusquely informed by a fur-coated individual (a munition-worker I decided later) that my favourite doss-house was now a Government Office.

Wearily I took counsel with my taxi-driver, and we eventually discovered an hotel which still posed as such and which could take me in. Exhausted with my labours, I implored my driver, who talked darkly of lack of petrol, to take me to S——'s for lunch. Dropping into my old corner seat, I looked round for my former waiter, and gloomily came to the conclusion that he must have been an alien enemy, as he was no longer present. Having finished my dozen oysters, to my horror I was informed I had expended the regulation three-and-six, and could have nothing more. Hastily I rushed round the corner to the T—— and completed my meal.

Having refreshed the inner man, I felt in a much more amiable frame of mind, and decided to go round to Ciro's, where I thought I would surely find many old friends. Memories of the incomparable *coon* band and joysome dances flashed through my mind, and I hastened my steps. Ciro's was still there, but how changed! In place of the fashionable bohemian club of former days, I found—a Y.M.C.A. canteen. Sadly retracing my footsteps, I heard a cheery cry—'That brings the war home to you, old thing,' and next moment was warmly shaking hands with a naval officer, one of my greatest friends.

As we strolled up Regent Street, I involuntarily saluted a gorgeous-looking individual whom I took to be a Marine officer of general rank, only to be covered with confusion when I was ironically informed by my companion that this stately personage was merely a cinema attendant. With that ease peculiar to the senior service, my friend piloted me through the gaping crowds into a narrow doorway, and climbing a steep stair, we were soon in a small room crowded with naval officers. 'Two Martinis, quick, please, Bobby, the Doc's had a shock and needs a pick-me-up,' was my introduction to this famous naval club.

My cares now vanished, and the remainder of my leave passed in a whirl of gaiety.

SERVICE COMMUNICATIONS

Service communications undoubtedly corrupt good manners, and are the direct cause of more bad language on the Western Front than anything else I know of. Imagine, for example, the members of a battalion headquarters sitting on a cold, misty night in a muddy trench, which is being actively bombarded by the enemy artillery, and which has nothing more substantial than a waterproof sheet to keep out rain, wind, and shells. A perspiring and breathless runner pushes his way in and hands to the adjutant a small envelope marked URGENT in block capitals. Thinking it is probably an operation order of supreme importance, it is opened amidst a breathless silence, and runs as follows:

To Peach AAA
Report immediately how many men in your battalion have a working knowledge of engines—turbine AAA Urgent AAA.

From Bawls AAA.

H—— murmurs the colonel; B—— F—— roars the major; S—O— B—— soliloquises the adjutant, as he resignedly lights another 'stinker' with the priceless document.

The time is 5.30 a.m. on a chilly April morning, the battalion is in its jumping-off trenches ready to go over the top at dawn. A runner dashes up with an envelope. Is this an order to cancel the operation, we wonder, and at the bottom of our hearts rather hope it is. Even the colonel, usually the coolest of individuals, shows some signs of excitement. He opens it and reads:

To Peach Medical AAA
Monthly enteric inoculation return not yet received. AAA Expedite AAA.

From Bawls Medical AAA.

At that moment our barrage opens and drowns our indignant protests.

Bairnsfather's famous picture of the raspberry-jam tins return is not merely the figment of a fertile imagination; such a situation can be seen any day on the Western Front. If you doubt my word, ask any adjutant or commanding officer of a battalion on active service.

During the Gallipoli evacuation I happened to lose a small book in which I jotted down weekly reports regarding the sanitary condition of the trenches. Six months later, sitting in a dugout on the Western Front, an envelope was handed to me by a breathless brigade orderly. It contained my long lost sanitary book, and also a pile of correspondence, showing that it had passed through the hands of twenty-six eminent staff officers, each of whom had added a short memo, as to what he considered the best method of finding the owner.

To the civilian this may appear a cumbersome method of procedure, but in reality it is eminently businesslike, and answers its purpose admirably, in so far as the individual concerned is always reached.

A Service 'memo' certainly differs entirely from the polite correspondence of commerce. It is curt and to the point. It passes through many hands, and all who come across it scribble something upon it. Some of the favourite additions are—'Passed to you, please.' 'For information and guidance.' 'For compliance.' 'For necessary action.' 'Noted and returned.' 'State reasons in writing.' 'Not approved.'

It is usual to have the battalion signal station in headquarters, and it is always interesting to hear the various messages in code and in clear which go through.

To the uninitiated every message would appear to be in code. For example, the following conversation takes place over the 'phone.

A. Hello, that R. Emma Beer?

B. Yipp.

A. Message.

B. Right.

A. Emma O R Emma Beer Ak Ak Ak Reference Beer Esses one three five oblique ten oblique sixteen section don para two Ak Ak Ak Return to reach this office at Blocks on Vron blocks off by three pip emma seven oblique two oblique seventeen Ak Ak Ak break Ak Don Emma Esses. Got it?

B. Yipp.

A. Cheer-oh— Rings off.

To the ordinary individual this is, of course, quite incomprehensible, but it is really quite simple, and when written down on the message form, reads:

M.O. R.M. Battalion Reference B.S. 135/10/16 section D, paragraph 2. Return to reach this office at Vron by 3 p.m. 7/2/17. A.D.M.S.

M. O., of course, stands for medical officer, and R. M. Battn. for Royal Marine Battalion. B.S. 135/10/16 is merely the reference number of a certain order issued by the A.D.M.S. (Assistant Director of Medical Services).

The English alphabet contains many letters which over the 'phone sound very similar. To prevent the possibility of any confusion, certain letters have special names. For example, A becomes Ak, B becomes Beer, D becomes Don, etc. Ak Ak Ak means a full stop, and 'break' means the end of the actual message. 'Blocks on' means 'use capital letters,' 'blocks off' 'cease using them.'

On one occasion I had to report on the medical fitness of a signaller for a commission. All went swimmingly until I came to the eye test, when he read off my types as Ak, Don, Beer, Esses, Emma, Toe, and then with profuse apologies corrected himself, and said A.D.B.S.M.T.

TABS AND TITLES

The whole world and his wife knows that 'Tabs' is the name given by the Tommy to those curious brands of cigarettes which are, from time to time, served out by a kindly and thoughtful government for the consumption of those who have a predilection for the soothing weed. They are also somewhat accurately described as 'stinkers,' 'ration fags,' 'bines,' or even by more opprobrious terms, but that is a digression. My purpose here is not to give a dissertation on the manifold evils of excessive devotion to my Lady Nicotine, but rather to make a few remarks, pertinent and otherwise, anent the many officers who wear 'Tabs' (or in military parlance 'lapels—two in number') of varying hue, and to briefly indicate the significance of these decorations.

Practically every officer attached to formations other than a battalion, who specialises even in a small way, wraps some coloured flannel round his hat, and adorns the lapels of his immaculate tunic with material of a similar shade, surmounted by a small gold button—all as is laid down in G.R.O. No. —— dated ——. He is even compelled to go further. In accordance with the immutable laws of the Medes and Persians, he also takes unto himself a string of letters which, to the uninitiated, arc both meaningless and bewildering. He entirely loses his own identity and camouflages himself under this new title, by which he is known and talked of by his friends and enemies alike.

Take, for example, the Ordnance Department—not that I have the slightest personal animosity against this most extraordinarily efficient branch of the Service, but merely to illustrate the point. The amiable gentleman who supplies the units of a division with everything from a field kitchen to a pair of socks wears an Oxford blue hatband and lapels of a similar colour. In addition, he rejoices in, and is known to all and sundry by the sobriquet of D.A.D.O.S. (pronounced Dados). This is not a term of endearment, as might be imagined, or even of opprobrium, but is his official designation, and being interpreted, means the Deputy Assistant Director of Ordnance Stores. His immediate superior on the corps staff is A.D.O.S., whilst the army possess a still more highly placed individual whom they affectionately term D.D.O.S. (D.-dos). This is not an after-dinner pronunciation, as one might think, but merely stands for the Deputy Director of Ordnance Stores. The highest functionary of all in the Ordnance Department is D.O.S. He lives, at least so I am credibly informed, somewhere in the purlieus of General Headquarters.

I possess a bowing acquaintance with two Dadoses; I have once seen an Ados, but D.-dos and Dos are still beyond my ken.

So it is throughout the whole army. Red tabs form the personal staff of our generals. Some make out schemes and direct operations. Others, like the A.P.M., look after our moral welfare; whilst the rest have each some particular function in assisting the successful progress of our mighty engine of war.

Those who wear blue tabs are too numerous to mention, and to attempt an accurate classification of the many other colours of tabs is too intricate to be interesting, and too uninteresting to serve any useful purpose.

In order fully to realise the intricacies of our army nomenclature, a journey must be made to the Western Front. A highly placed official at Whitehall gives the traveller hasty instructions to report to the R.T.O. at Charing Cross, the M.L.O. at Folkestone, his opposite number at Boulogne, the D.A.D.R.T. at St. Pol, and suggests that the M.F.O. may be persuaded to arrange about the baggage. On reaching his destination a M.F.P. directs him to D.H.Q. and he interviews the G.S.O.I., who details a runner to take him to the A.A. and Q.M.G. From there he is sent to the D.A.Q.M.G., who tells him he should not have reported to 'Q' branch at all, but to the A.D.M.S. With infinite difficulty he locates the habitation of this dignitary, only to find he is not at home. However, he finally runs the D.A.D.M.S. to ground, who orders him to go to Don 27 Beer 45, telling him that, if he be lucky, he may pick up an M.L. or G.S. wagon on the road, and on arrival he should ask the B.T.O. to send a half limber for his baggage.

This somewhat obscure map reference is eventually discovered and found to be a Brigade H.Q. The G.O.C. and B.M. 'X.' Brigade are in the trenches, the S.C. is busy, but the B.I.O. and B,B,0. are finally found. The former being a man of parts at once appreciates the wanderer's ignorance of Service matters and invites him to have a stiff B. and S. (the only abbreviation he has as yet fully understood), and tells off a runner to guide him to the battalion he has been ordered to join. He finally reaches Battn. H.Q. *via* a tortuous C.T., and the CO. makes him an admirer for life by giving him a little more much-needed liquid refreshment, showing him his R.A.P. and promising to arrange with the T.O. and Q.M. to get his valise sent up.

That night at dinner the novice attempts to show an intelligent appreciation of the delinquencies of the Toe Emmas, the D.M.G.O., the A.P.M., the S.S.O., the —— heavies, etc., etc., as volubly expressed by an irate adjutant, and finally falls asleep only to dream of unending strings of letters, and yards of coloured flannel of varying hue.

Only a Casualty

In the lounge of the Savoy all was laughter and merriment—the only sign of war a few figures in khaki or blue and gold. Sitting in my comfortable chair, I wondered when she would come, and ran over in my mind for the hundredth time how I could describe to her the manner of his death. It was only last week that we were walking along that shallow bit of trench when a German sniper got him in the chest. Such an everyday affair. I'd seen it happen hundreds of times before, but somehow or other it seemed different when it was one's best pal who was lying in the mud slowly bleeding to death, and our vaunted medical science could do nothing to save him.

We carried him back to my aid post and there he died, his last thoughts and his last words all of her. Next day we buried him, sticking in the ground a flimsy wooden cross with his name rudely scrawled upon it. Just another officer killed. It makes no difference to the war. The guns still thunder as usual and all is outwardly the same, but I have lost my best pal, and the girl I'm waiting for has a blank in her life which can never be filled.

The Chaplain

In peace time many of us only knew clergymen in a more or less perfunctory way. We now know them better, and the more we see of them, the more we appreciate them. From time to time the newspapers quote the bald and somewhat uninteresting official description of how Chaplain IV. Class ——won the V.C., D.S.O., or M.C., but rarely do the people at home fully appreciate what the work of a battalion padre is. Many of my readers will recall how a certain Roman Catholic priest won the D.S.O. at Beaucourt. To see this venerable, white-haired old man, spectacles on the point of his nose, his legs clothed in gumboots, stumbling through trenches waist-deep in mud, to some point in the front line where the shelling was heaviest, and hence the casualties greatest, was always an example to all.

His creed was that a man wants to see his priest *before* he is dead, and though my religion is not his, I can testify to the truth of his statement and to the fact that he lived up to it. A few words whispered in a severely wounded man's ear by his priest are almost magical in effect. An ineffable change appears on his face, he thinks no more of his wounds, death has now no terrors for him, and he passes into the great hereafter content and uncomplaining, at peace with all the world and fit to meet his Maker.

The Souvenir Hunter

Bairnsfather's famous picture of Alf sitting astride an enormous projectile attempting to remove the fuse cap, whilst his companion helpfully remarks, 'Hit 'im 'ard, they usually fizzes afore they goes off,' tends to remind us of the inherent desire of us all for souvenirs. This craze is found all the world over. I am credibly informed that the cannibal treasures some portion of the unfortunate missionary he has devoured as a visible memory of his tasty repast. I believe that a certain wealthy American wished to remove the Nelson monument to his yankee home as a memento of his visit across the water. Not infrequently has one of the so-called weaker sex ruthlessly torn a button from my immaculate tunic to add to her already enormous collection, but never have I come across such an inveterate souvenir hunter as the British Tommy.

Has any one of them had a bullet or shell fragment removed from his interior which he does not treasure with the utmost care? How many men have risked their lives in order to become the proud possessor of a helmet of the Prussian Guard, or a bayonet with a saw edge? Duty, however, comes before pleasure, and many of us have often had to forgo the joy of adding to our collections, owing to our energies being needed for more serious affairs. Lieutenant A. P. Herbert of the R.N.D. expresses our sentiments well in his poem *Sooveneers*.

SOOVENEERS[1]

(A Song of Wisdom)

When pore old Fritz is boosted out
'E leaves 'is goods be'ind,
And the boys go 'unting round about
To see what they can find.

For pistols and for funny pipes
To give their grateful wives T
hey lose their 'eads, they lose their 'ipes,
And then they lose their lives.

Ah, do not seek no sooveneer
When you 'ave took the village.
Though there is 'eaps of Fritz's gear
And Prussian 'ats to pillage:
But make you ready for the brute
Or out of it 'e'll shove you,
And you may 'ave some lovely loot,
But General 'Aig won't love you.

There's 'elmets and there's furbelows.
And buttons is not bad,
But if you must 'ave meementoes
There's better to be 'ad:
A golden stripe is easy got.
Likewise the D.C.M.,
And Duggie will not have you shot
If you go 'ome with them.

So do not seek, etc.

But I will take some poppy-seed
To plant in our backyard,
And teach us all to take more 'eed
Of actions which is barred:
For poppies everywhere appears
O'er them 'oo died in sin,
'Oo would go 'unting sooveneers
Instead of digging in.

So we will seek no sooveneer
When we 'ave took the village.

---

1. Quoted by permission of the Editor of *Mudhook*.

Though there is 'eaps of Fritz's gear
And Prussian 'ats to pillage:
But take 'is tools and dig like 'Ell,
Or out of it 'e'll shove us,
And we shall lose our loot as well
And nobody will love us.

A GOOD SOUVENIR.

It is our earnest hope that those unlucky individuals who have returned home unfit for further fighting and without a souvenir to remind them of those eventful days they spent with the Royal Naval Division will find this book recalls a few memories of their experiences of active service either at Antwerp, in Gallipoli, Greece, or France, or perhaps on all these fronts.

THE PEN IS MIGHTIER THAN THE SWORD.

Printed in August 2023
by Rotomail Italia S.p.A., Vignate (MI) - Italy